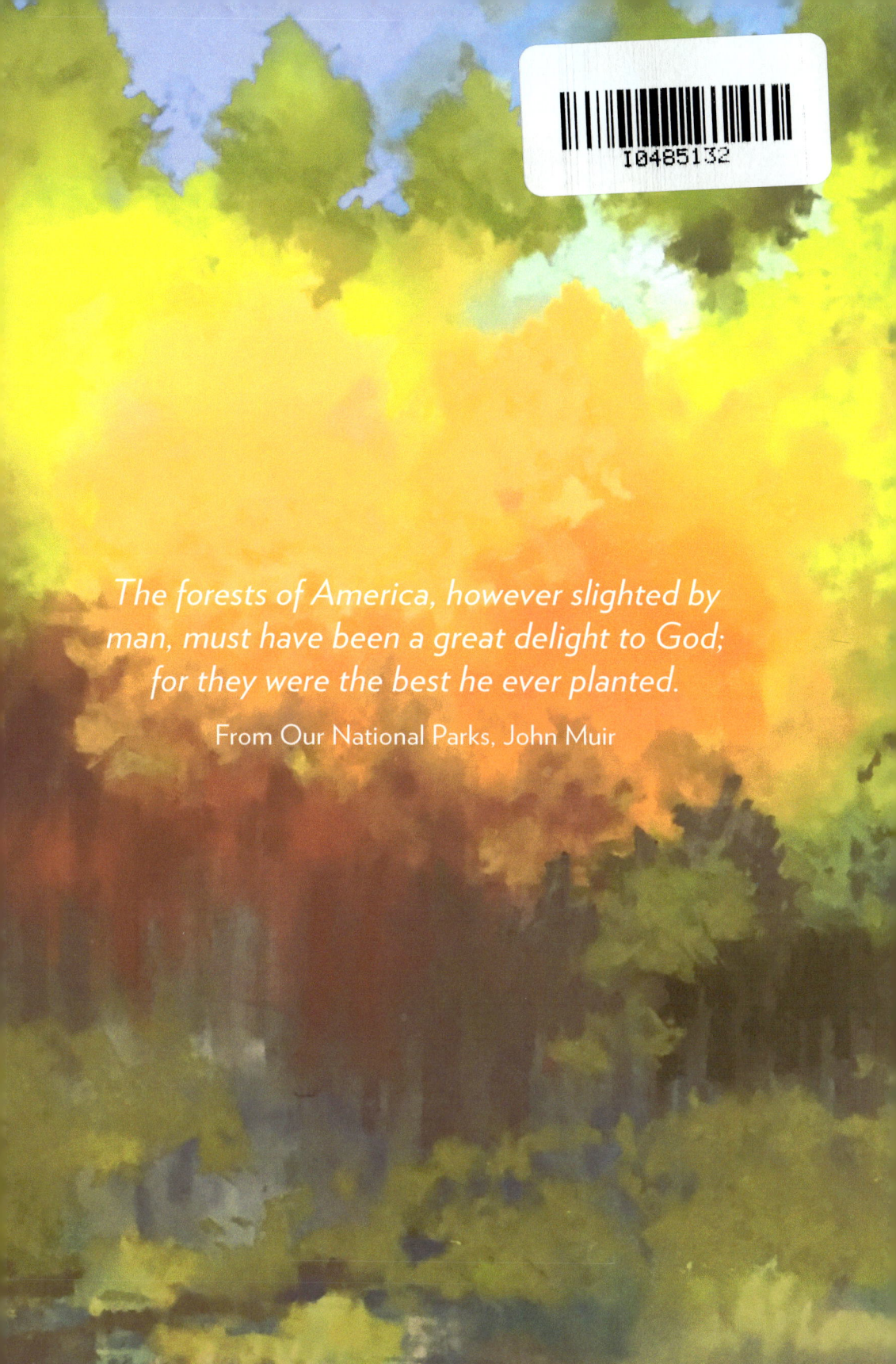

The forests of America, however slighted by man, must have been a great delight to God; for they were the best he ever planted.

From Our National Parks, John Muir

Green Pigment Publications
Falls Church, Virginia

When Color Is The Subject
Pastels Are Bold

Written and Illustrated by Alexia Scott, MFA

ISBN-13:978-0-9915547-4-4 Published by Alexia Scott

Discover other titles by Alexia Scott:
Pastel Painting Is Transcendental

Contact: Alexia Scott, alexiapaints@gmail.com
http://www.alexiascott.com

On my website there are many pastel paintings and oil paintings. After finishing this book, feel free to try your hand at using any of my images as reference for your next pastel painting. Eventually, we want you outside enjoying nature and painting on your own.

Artwork & Photography: Alexia Scott
Project Editor: Linda Scott
Marketing Director: Alexandra Koury
Book Design: Marinda Scott

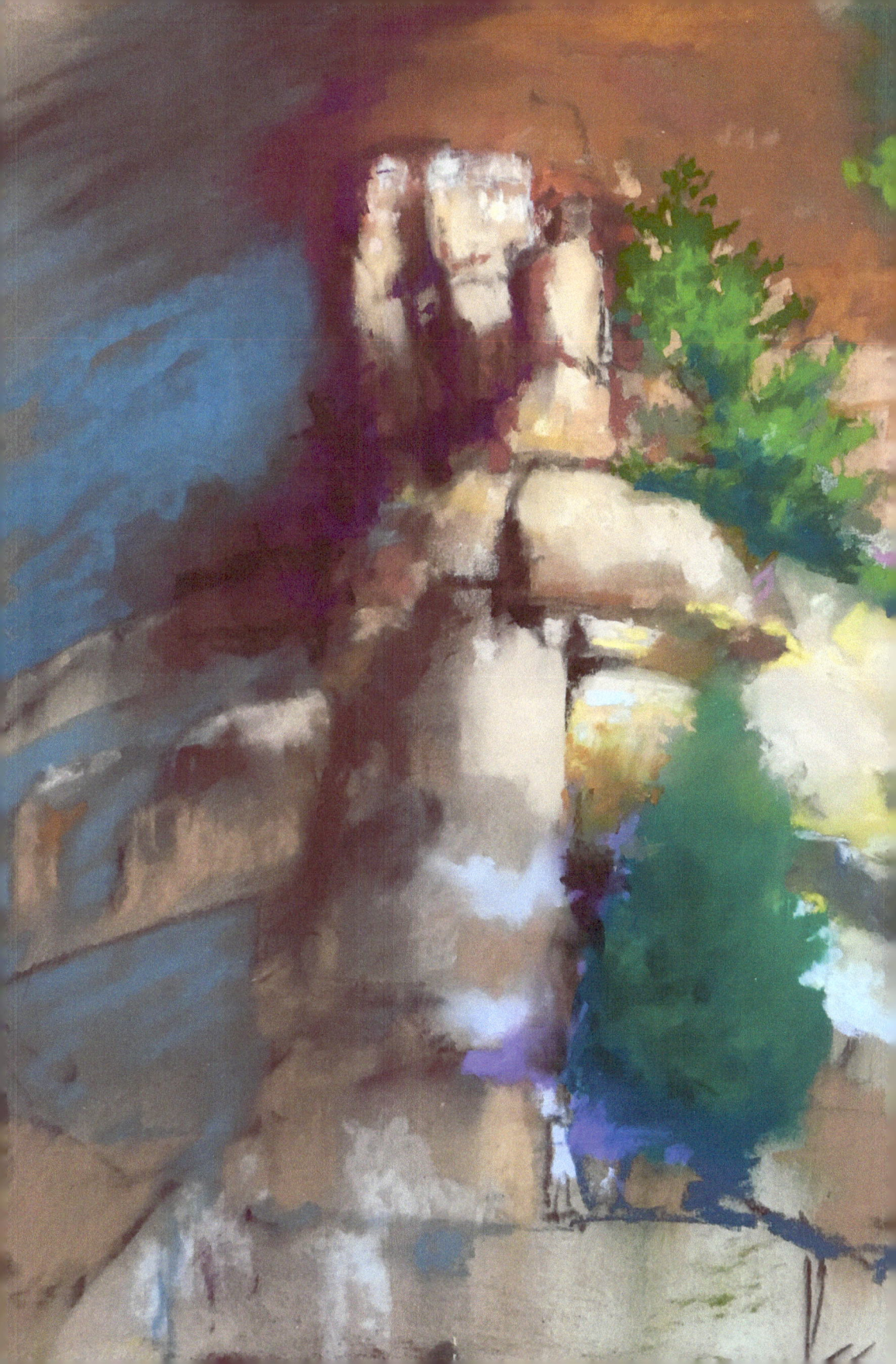

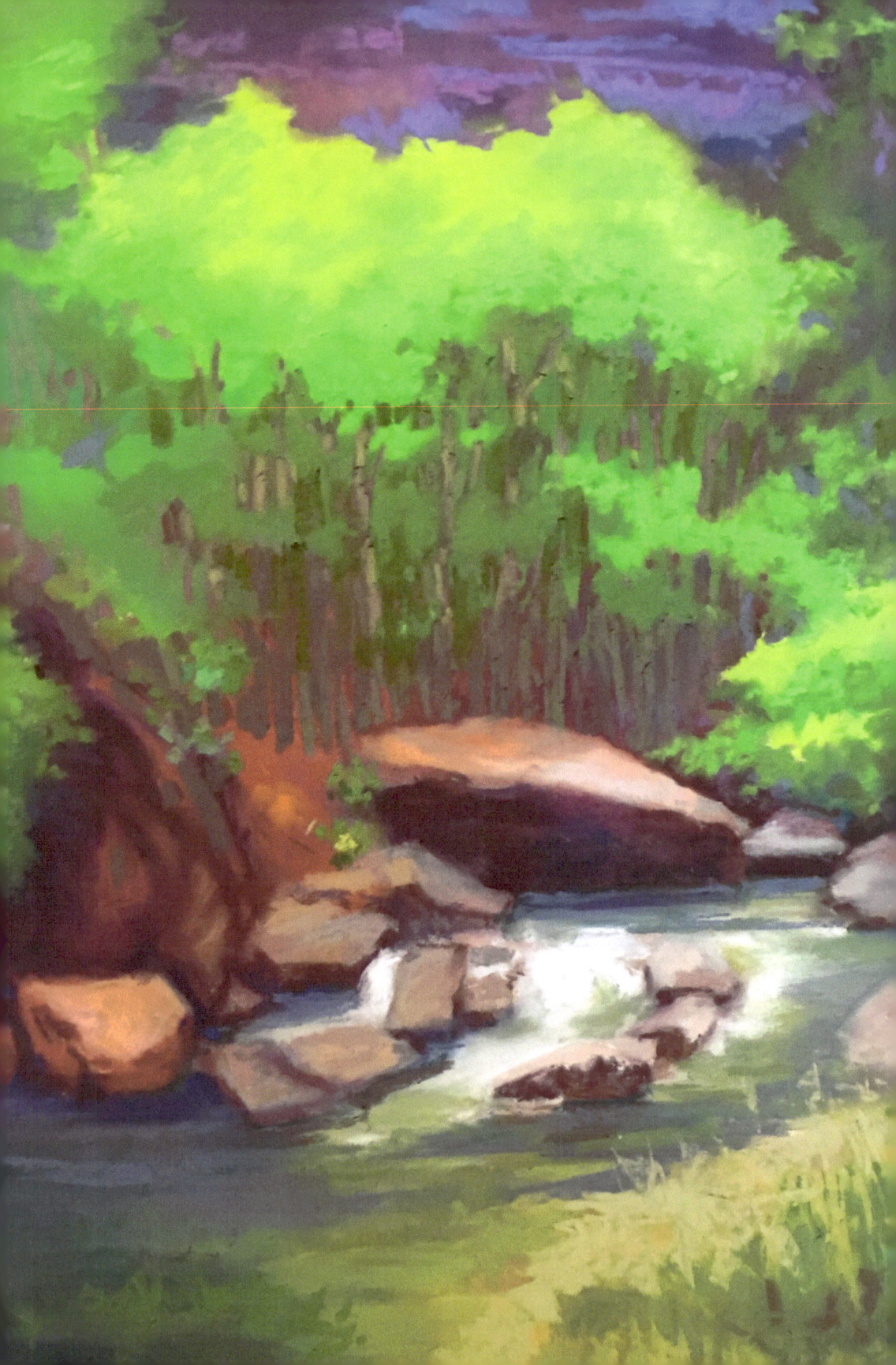

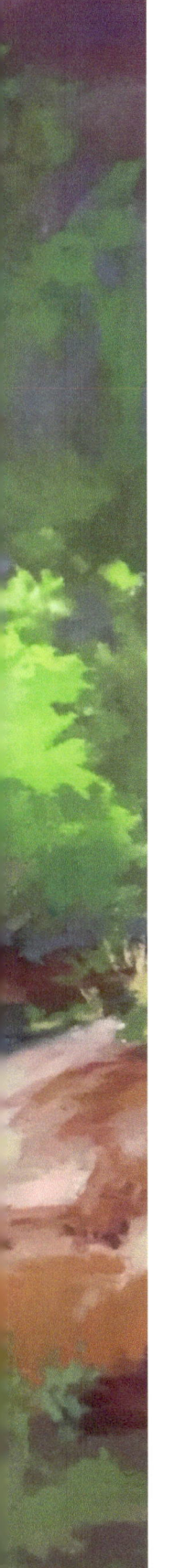

When Color is the Subject

PASTELS ARE BOLD

By Alexia Scott, MFA

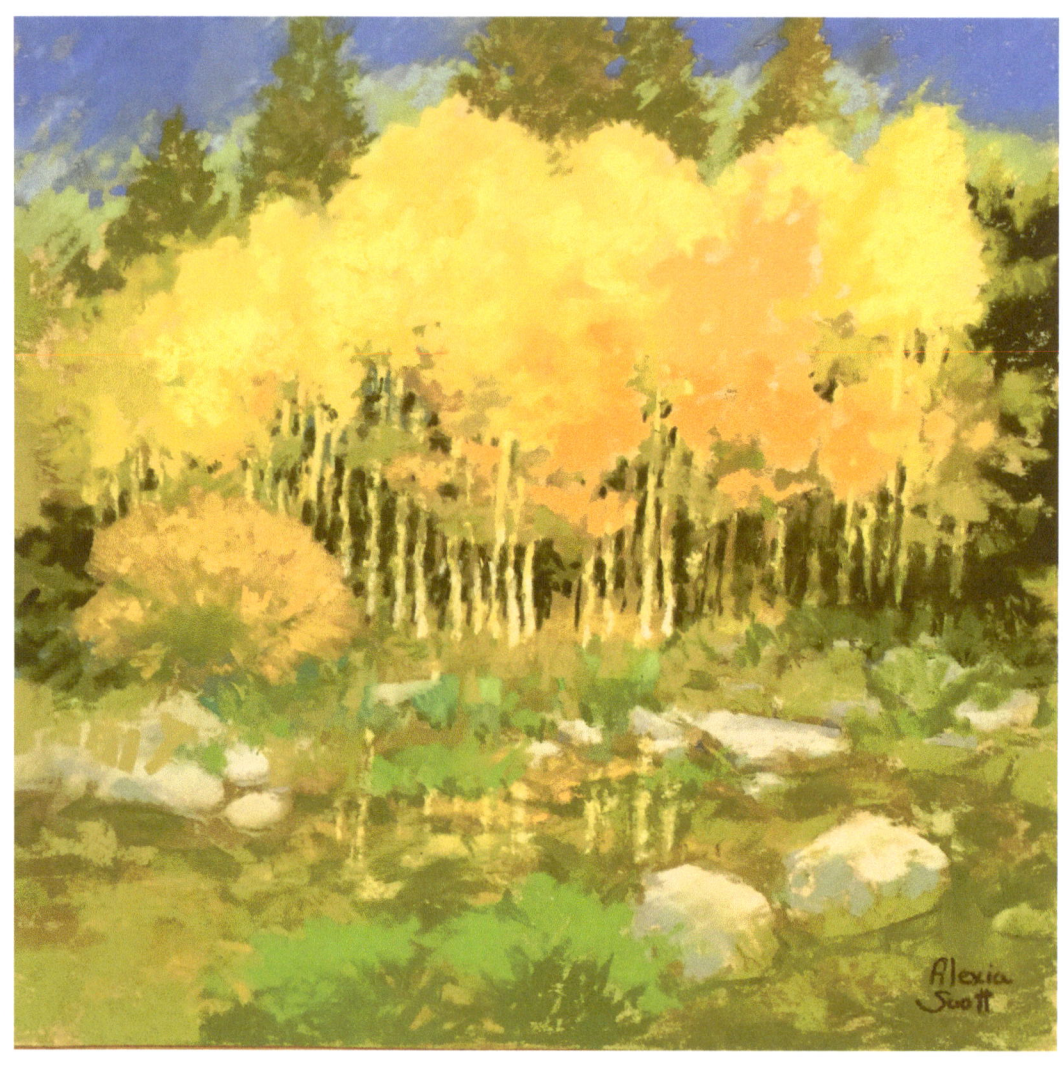

High Plateau Aspen, pastel on pastel board, 12" x 12", Duck Creek, Utah, 9/25/17. Sitting on a rock, the warmer afternoon sun on my back, I sketched this view as a preliminary study for a larger painting. I prefer to start on location; sometimes one study will begin a series of paintings. The Aspen in the upper plateau area, where our cabin was located, turned beautiful fall colors during our visit. High Plateau Aspen inspired this book.

Table of Contents

Preface: Copy and Learn Pastels 9

A Little Art History 13

We Need Color 14

Why Landscapes 17

    Supplies 17

Demo: September Aspen at Duck Creek Utah, 2017 18

    The Beginning 20

    Soft Pastel Brands 33

Design Your Painting 38

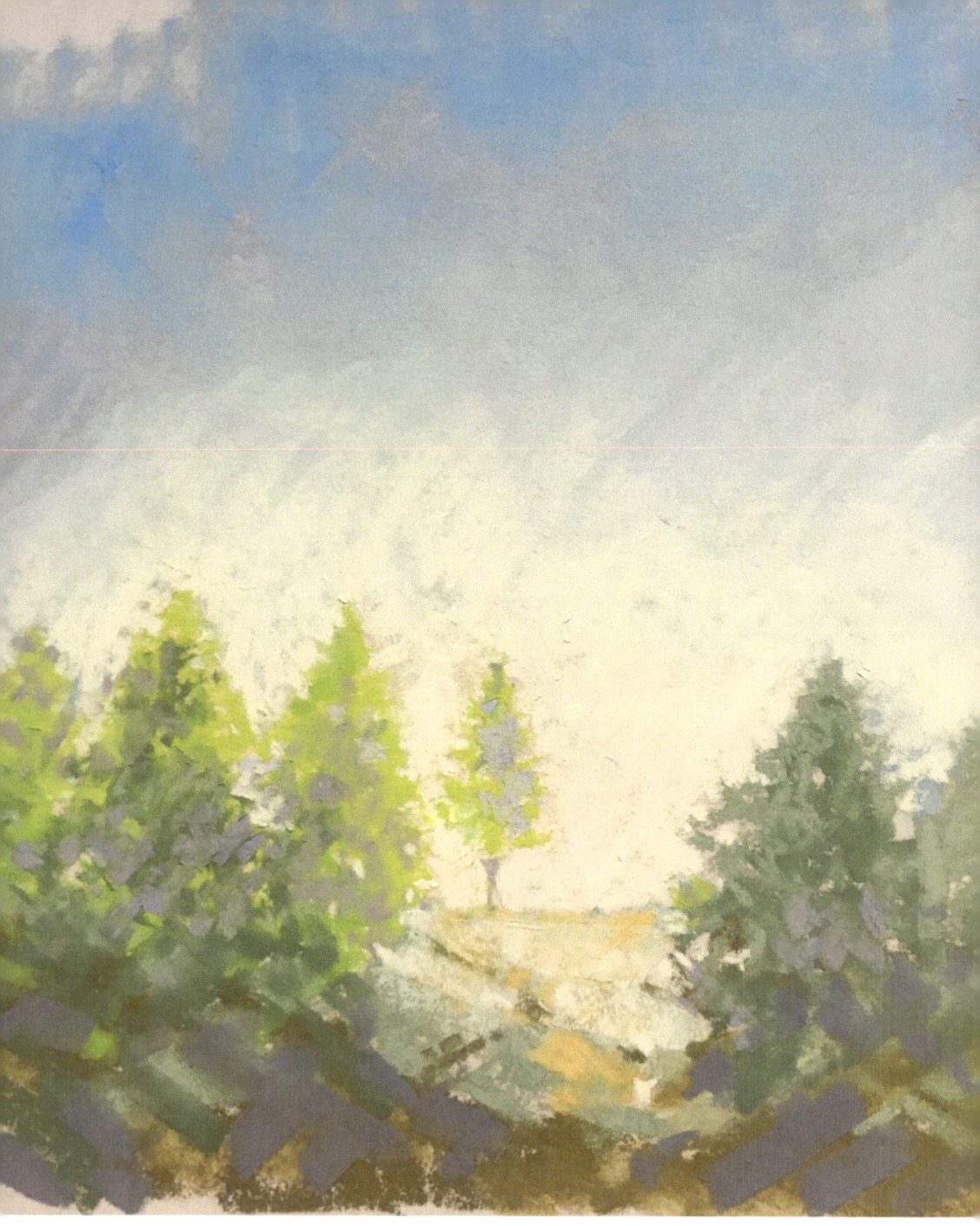

Frosty Utah Morning, pastel on pastel board, 8"x 8", 9/22/17 by Alexia Scott. The view painted from my car window, it was sunrise and 14 degrees.

Copy and Learn Pastels

Learning is something we should do throughout our lives, and learning about painting is something to be shared. There are different ways to make a pie and there are just as many ways to paint with pastels. What you already know is not wrong, just add it to what you learn here. It is the combinations of knowledge which give us our distinctive look in art. Instead of joining a book club, start a pastel painting club! There will be many paths to find your look. The goal here is learning. Pastels are very portable. You can work on your lap in your home or with a group where you can encourage each other. Like reading a book, begin at home and on your own. Meet once a month with your group and bring your work. All the work will look different. What I love about teaching is seeing the students' own self become part of their work. This is honest art because you are studying, trying, learning, and doing. I believe to be an artist, you need to feel that you have expanded knowledge and that is why I like to add history to my work. This makes you richer in knowledge and ability. This is something to be explored, not hastily achieved.

For centuries, in the education of artists around the world, students copied the work of their master teacher and other artists' work in the galleries. While I was in graduate school, I spent a year coping my favorite artists at the National Gallery of Art in Washington, D.C. This was very enjoyable and fulfilling. There was no need to be creative. The original artist had done that so I would be free to simply look at his/her process, colors, and surface brushstrokes and analyze what it was that drew me to the painting. I have always worked alongside my students while demonstrating how to get started and where to go from there. It is their job to stick with it and finish. This is how you learn.

There are many paths to creating and no real right or wrong direction, but there is a process that can be helpful. When you copy a painting that appeals to you, analyze why you were drawn to it. The creative process is a personal experience so the guidelines and images of my process are for guidance. Use what appeals to you and do not hesitate to deviate. No matter how careful you are at copying your painting, it will ultimately be your own work to display and enjoy.

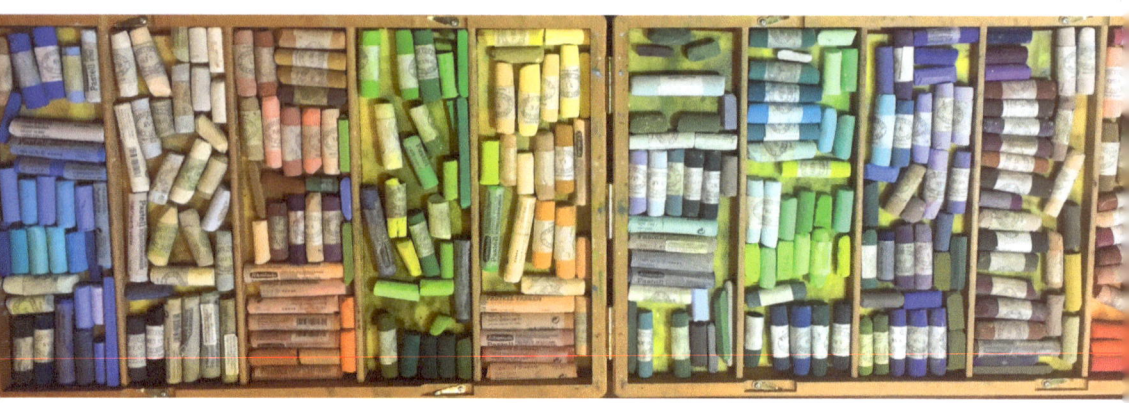

When Color is the Subject

The history of color, its psychological effects, the "how" and "why" artists choose their colors, and the production history of the pigments we use all come into play when the artist explores their options. The artist must decide how close to reality or how inventive their color choices will be for their work and their style.

As we thumb through the long past of man-made art, we see naturalistic colors based on available pigments. Our early drawings of earth tones made from minerals ground and mixed with animal fats, represent imagery the artist wanted to present. The line drawings of animals and humans are narrative in nature and not dependent on the color of the line. If you are drawing a mushroom with a brown line or a purple line, it still looks like a mushroom.

This color process takes time for the artist and should not be rushed. The most important element is to experiment with many methods and styles that attract you. Each path you take improves the others. You can't lose. You only lose by not working.

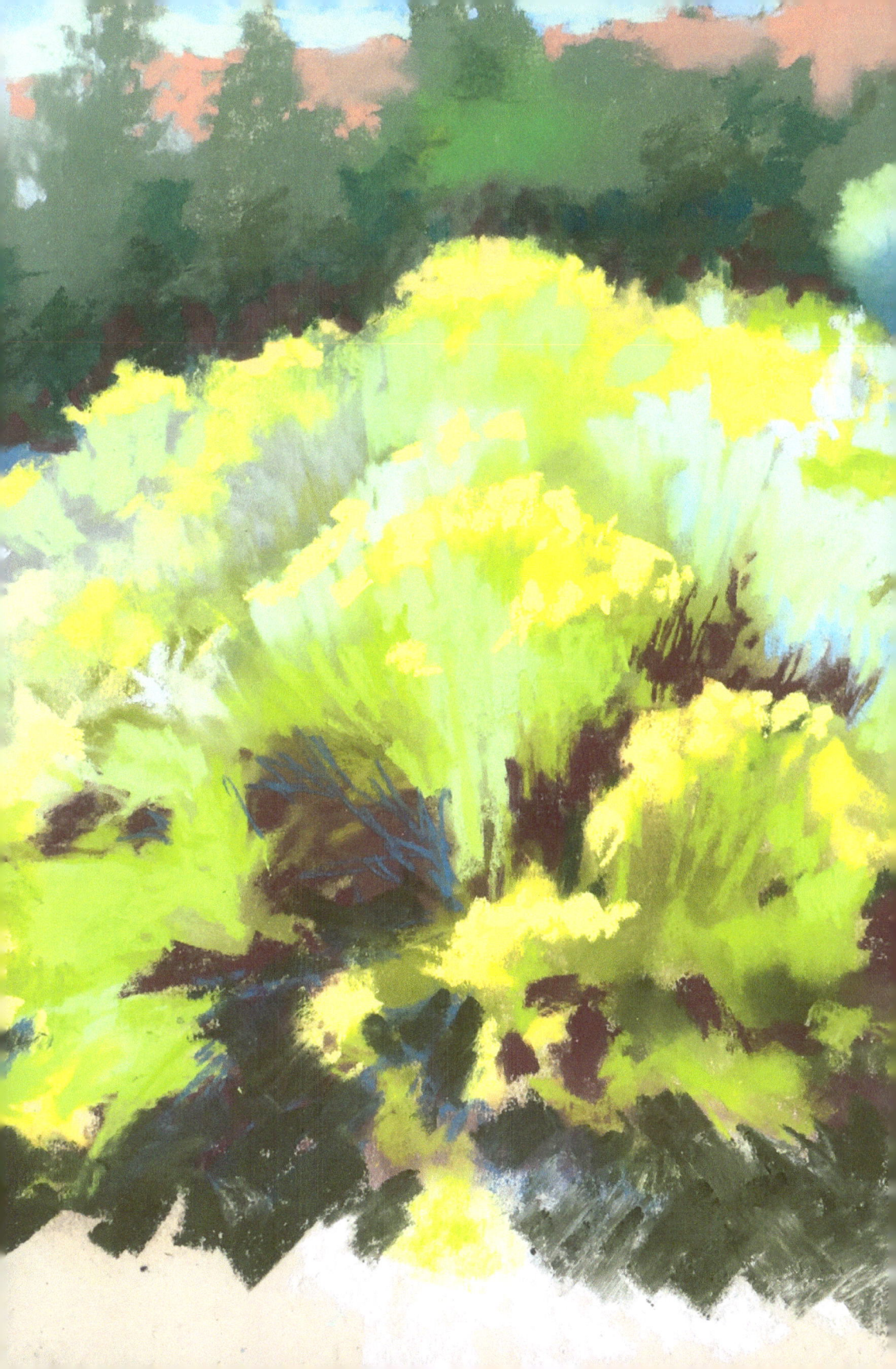

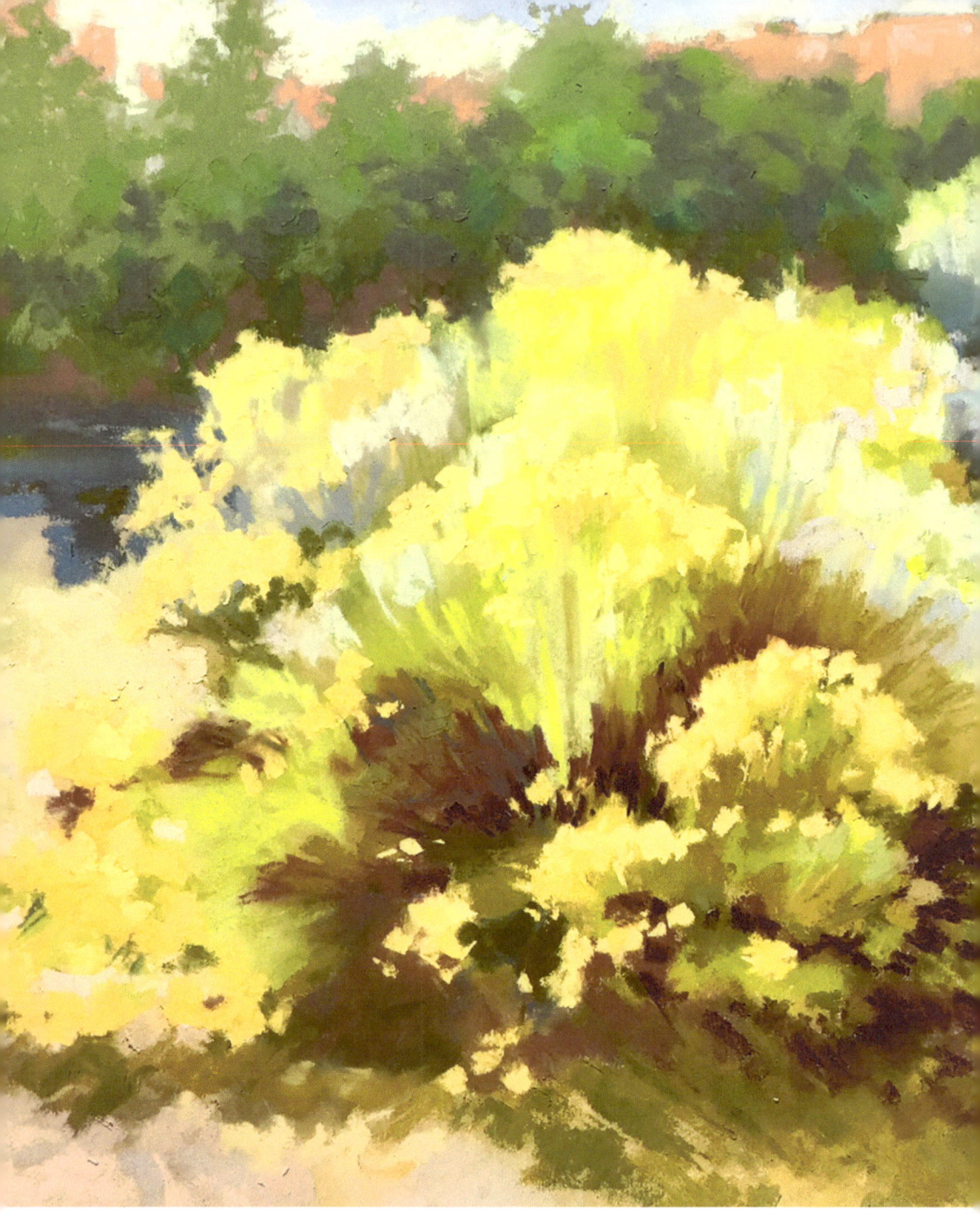

Campsite Wildflower, pastel on pastel board, 12" x 12", 9/23/17 by Alexia Scott, painted from my car. I visited this site two days to paint the red rocks. On my return visit, a big camper was in the spot so I painted the flower.

A Little Art History

One of the earliest artistic movements where color takes center stage is Mannerism. This style of artificial color, elongated figures, and unusual unbalanced composition announced a new freedom from naturalism that the artists explored. Mannerism emerged in Italy and Europe in general around the year 1520 and lasted about 60 years. Most art historians agree that through the ages religion was a driving force within the artists to create, not politics or war or our daily needs, but the desire to praise God.

Mannerism and its artistic freedoms coincide with and is a result of several historic events that upended the theological understanding of that time in Europe, the Reformation and the Printing Press. On October 31, 1517, Martin Luther, a monk and professor of theology at the University of Wittenberg nailed his 95 theses or topics to debate with the Church on the doors of All Saints' Church in Wittenberg. The Reformation became essentially a freedom in Christianity, freedom to pray to God without a priest to intercede on your behalf, and the printing press providing printed material and the freedom of learning. It was also a time of polarized feelings and great turmoil and greater anger.

The unusual color of the mannerist style is the first thing I notice when I look at the work of the painters from this movement. Jacopo Pontormo's Entombment from 1528 explodes with bright warm colors that draw you toward the painting. You see the color first and realize the sad event second. Art historians claim that the style developed because the High Renaissance had solved all the technical problems in manipulating light and shade to produce the necessary imagery to illustrate scripture. Artists illustrated scripture for the church because literacy was very low and a picture was communication. However, I feel this movement in painting was more of a reaction to the new freedoms the Reformation was adding to the timeline of art history. It was a time when the artist began to feel free to be more expressive and a desire to share their own vision of these events in scripture. Patrons were not solely limited to the church. Religious expression was still the moving force and subject. This actually allowed color to be the subject of the painting.

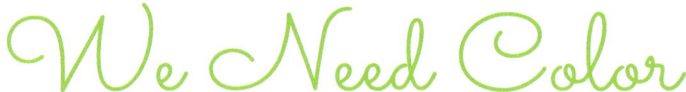

We Need Color

It is possible that the process of study that generated the new color came from the Mannerist artists' desire to express this new time in an emotional way. Experiencing both confusion and exaltation being consumed by the complexities of color was therapeutic. Color is complicated.

The complexities of color are a unique quality of this element of art and you actually know more color theory than you think you know. With very little effort, you will become enlisted in discovering the endless possibilities for your creative work. There are a few guidelines: cool colors recede, warm colors come forward. Color is relative to its surroundings; the same color will look different depending what it is next to on the picture plane. Color can change your mood and consume your thoughts while you are at work on your pastel painting. Pastels are the very best way to explore the intricacies of color. By picking colors rather than mixing colors you look at the pigments in a different way, often choosing something you would never have mixed. With a large box of pastels in hand, just the look of them will make you smile.

A well thought-out painting will take into consideration all the basic elements of art, but only allow one element to dominate each work. As a review, these elements are line, shape, form, value, space, texture, and color. When you choose form, it is generally the object you are interested in such as a drawing of your friend across the table or just the table with an object on it to draw your attention. In order to go a step further, the artist can choose to express a feeling. Or, the artist can choose to paint a location and work from their memory of a sight that filled them with happiness, a place they want to share with others. It might always mean more to the artist than the viewer, but the process the artist relives is definitely uplifting.

I like to start on location and choose my element by the first thought that comes to mind when I see the view. I live in Virginia, a very beautiful state. However, new landscapes spark innovation and inspiration. On a recent trip to Utah, I imagined I would paint red rocks but instead was stunned by the yellow Aspen. They are a unique living thing and required more than just a representation; they ask for an impression. They quiver and are bold in color in the fall. Each morning I worked for a couple of hours on location in different places to study the landscape. Remember, that without light, or diminished light, there is little color. Therefore, if you love color, you should wait until the sun is up and bright.

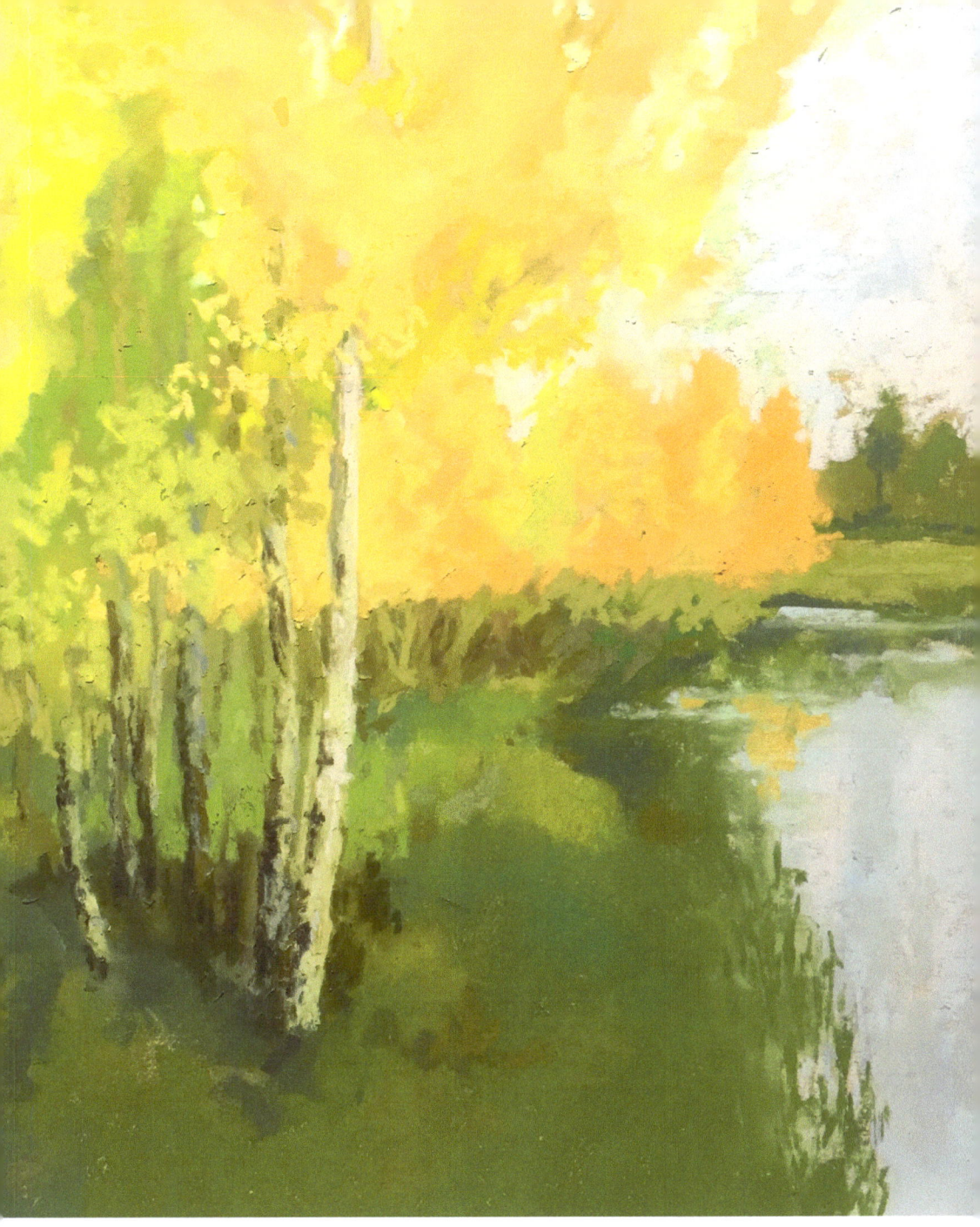

Duck Creek Aspen, First Color, pastel on pastel board, 12"x 12" started on 9/25/17 in Utah, completed in Virginia. The overcast day changes the colors. However, the warm yellows still draw us in to the view and the deep verdant green grasses frame the splendor.

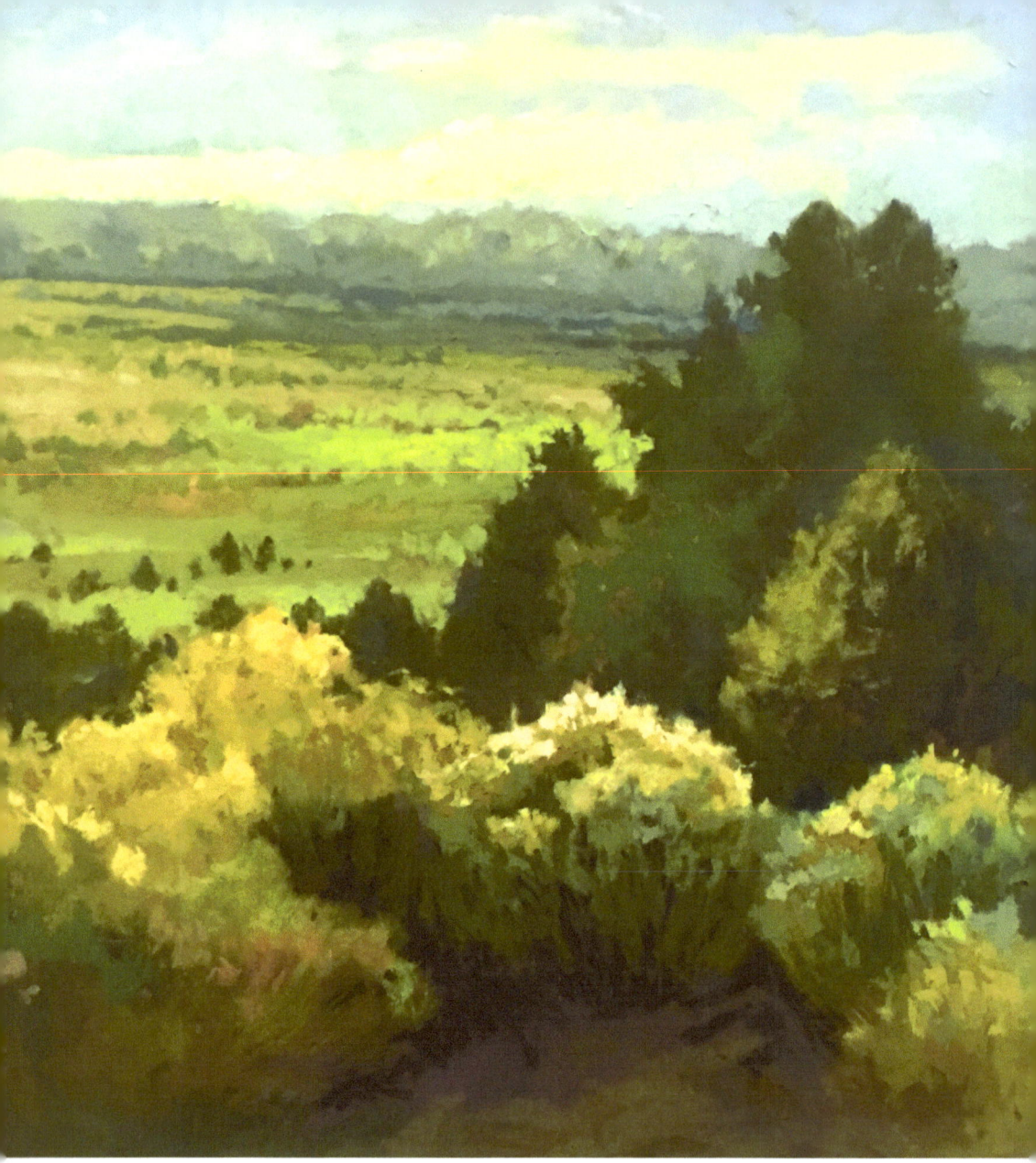

Morning Across the Valley, pastel on pastel board, 16" x 20", 9/24/17, Utah

The weather turned very cold for this morning painting. It was necessary to sit in my car and paint at an overlook of the valley near Bryce Canyon. The sun is just up and the light is diminished; it is 25 degrees outside. Each morning, I started a new painting to take back home to finish. When you are in the studio and away from the view, your knowledge of painting light and form aids in creating your piece. By copying paintings, you are developing your own set of color files in your head. Learning painted imagery will eventually encourage your creativity. The only way to learn to paint is to paint.

Why Landscapes

Landscape painting wasn't really a separate genre in painting until the 17th and 18th centuries when science and the natural world became a thing to study. Spending time with nature, the establishment of public parks such as Boston's Common, parts of which date back to 1728, show the changing priorities of our citizens. The art world, always reflective of society, began to paint landscapes as subjects. The artists made great excursions to exotic places. The allure of the landscape as a subject for artists is its never-ending source of inspiration and visual flexibility. You can start with what is out in nature in front of you, and since you are working on location in pastels, you never have what you want and are forced from the beginning to be creative. Don't try to copy exactly. Enjoy yourself and be expressive. Use my work as a guide, not a blueprint.

SUPPLIES

Pastels are pure pigment in stick form. They are opaque and there are hundreds to choose from. From the start, you will find that pastels force you to be creative and experiment with different colors. Don't try to copy exactly. This lesson is not paint by numbers or paint with wine; it is the same instruction I shared with my college students. This pastel painting began in Utah and was completed in my studio back in Virginia. It took about a week, so don't feel you should complete your work in one night.

If you are a beginner, don't work too large at first. Invest in a large box of Gallery Semi-hard pastels by **Mungyo** (student grade) or Prismacolor NuPastels. These are artist-grade semi-hard sticks. You can also go to your local art store and pick out the colors for this painting, one pastel stick at a time. The NuPastels are designed for conceptualizing. Designers used to use them before computers took over. I buy from *www.dakotapastels.com* and *www.jerrysartarama.com*. Take a look at what they have. I also use Uart 400 grit sanded paper which you can get in a 9" x 12" pack, or whatever size you want to make your painting. This paper holds the pastel pigment and allows for many layers of work as you refine your image. A soft paintbrush is useful for reducing pastel build up.

If you are not working too large, you can place a towel over your lap and work (no need for an easel or extra equipment). I often do this out in the field. There is a danger in elongating your image but the trees won't care. You will also need an old hand towel for your fingers. I don't limit myself to one set of pastels; that is just to get you started. Different brands have closely related colors that are helpful in the more detailed areas of your work.

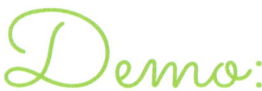

Demo:

SEPTEMBER ASPEN AT DUCK CREEK, UTAH, 2017
Pastel on pastel board, 16" x 20" by Alexia Scott

These images taken with my iPhone are a record of my working process. They have not been altered so you will see messy places where I laid pastels on my board and made marks. I doodled around gesture drawing to find my space within my picture plane edges and I wasn't worried about mistakes and you shouldn't be either. This first gesture drawing will be an outline for your composition. Don't be too neat and don't try to copy exactly. Just as I used the Utah landscape as reference, you can do the same with my images. Because this scene is lit from the back, the trees are patches of color rather than an expression of volume. I chose this view because of its abstract quality and lack of reliance on volume and it expresses our subject of color.

First determine your horizon line where your eye looks straight ahead. I was down the hill from this clump of trees so their beauty was bright and bold over my head and my sight looked low and forward peeking through the silhouetted tree trunks. When your subject is lit from the back, the volume of the trees is not evident. The Aspen tree cluster before you are patches of color. You will need the tree trunks to announce their identity.

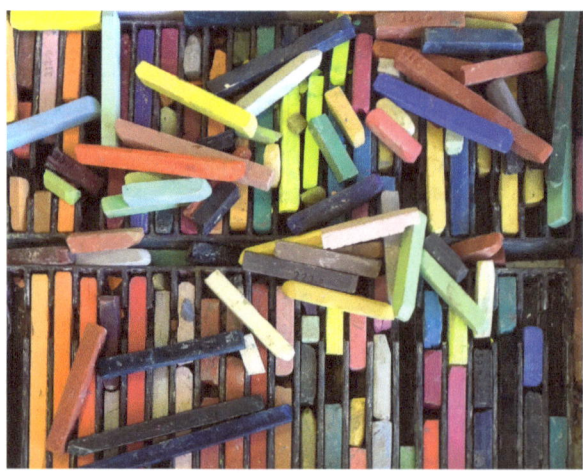

Prismacolor NuPastels

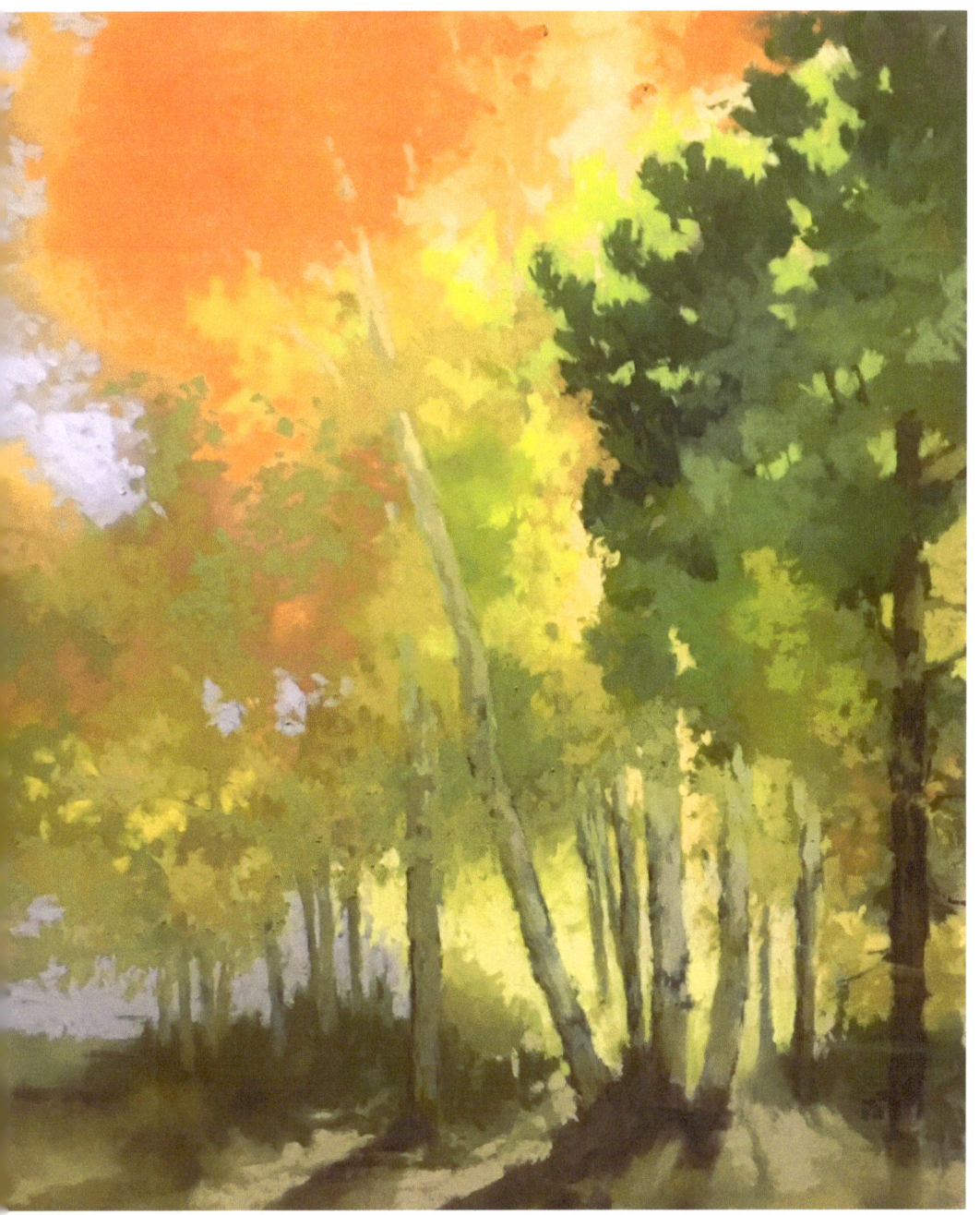

THE BEGINNING

I always start with the pastel sticks. When traveling, sometimes that is all I have with me. You can do a great deal with a box of pastels and pad of pastel paper. I always keep these in my car. I also love to oil paint, but the heat and cold are damaging to the paint if you leave them in the car.

Pastel painting is different from pastel drawing because you handle the pastels more like a paintbrush rather than a pencil. Use the corner to draw a line and the flat edge to make broader paint-like strokes. If you want an even broader stroke, break the pastel and use a piece one inch long. You can mix all the different brands of dry pastels but not with the oil pastels. Allow your pastel painting to look like a pastel.

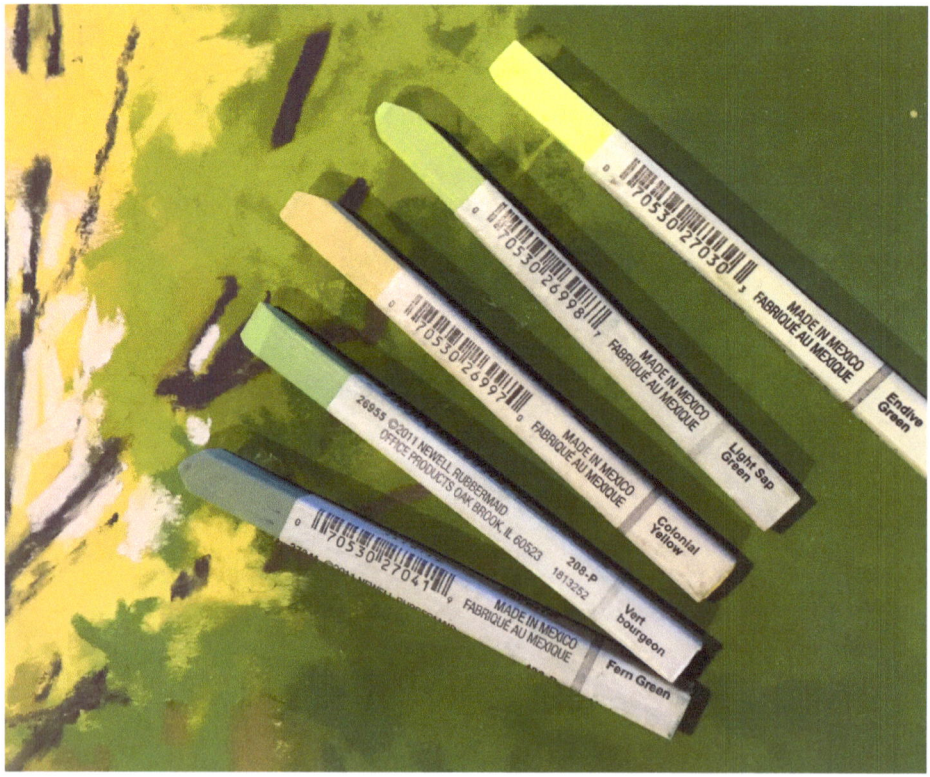

Color, color, color. Think of this first and throughout your work. Don't draw the spring green with a point but turn your pastel on its side, a piece about one-half of an inch and scribble. Use the square end like a paintbrush. Pastels are opaque and can cover each other so you don't have to be careful — be expressive. Begin as an abstraction, without detail just color and a vague form suggesting the overall shape of the sunlit leaves.

Choose an orange for the autumn leaves. We want to cover our space with intent. It looks random but is not.

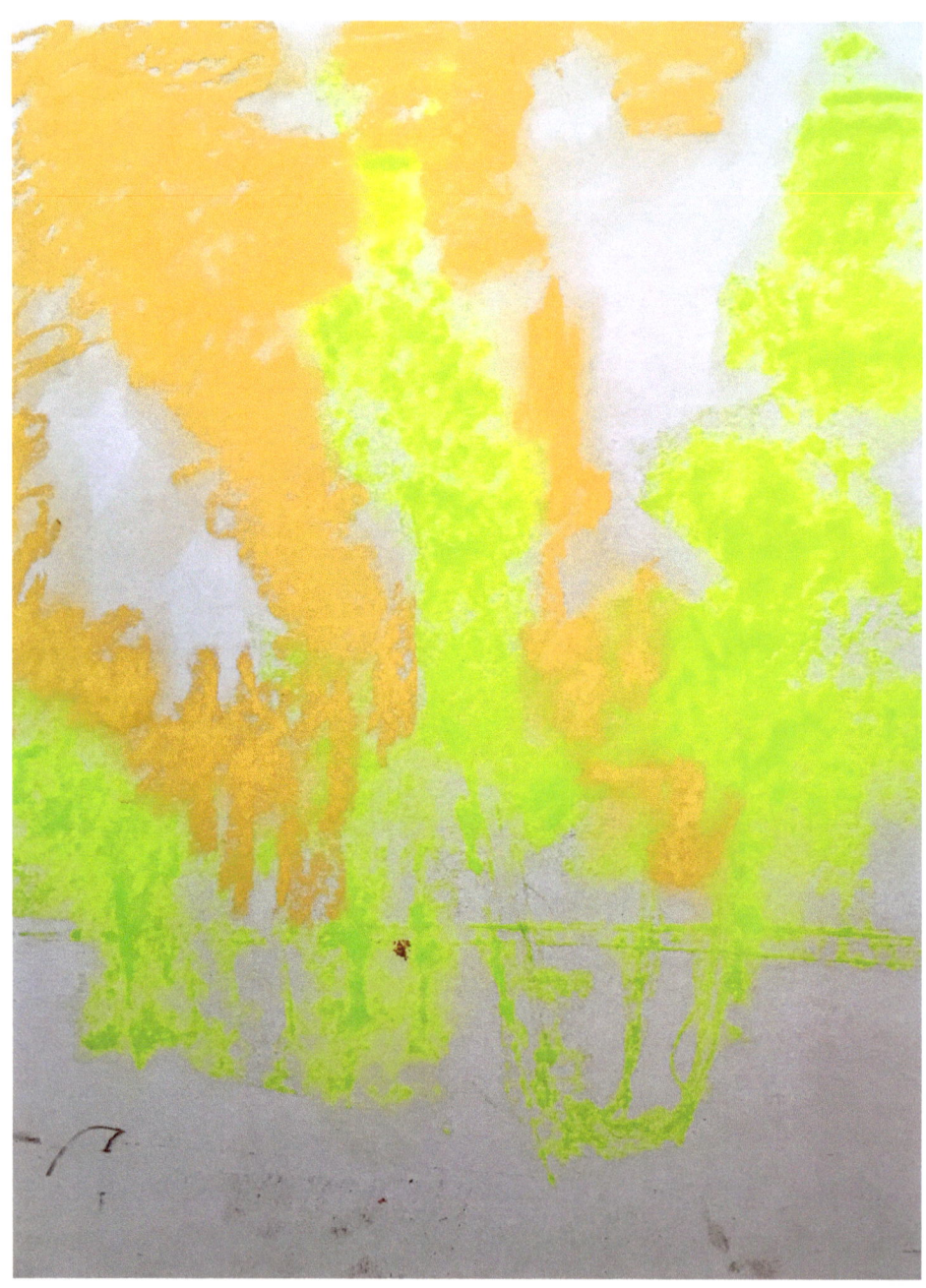

Asymmetrical balance. This cluster of Aspen has overlapping branches. Notice the darker orange toward the ground line. This adds weight and anchors the composition. Continue to think vertical; make some vertical markings.

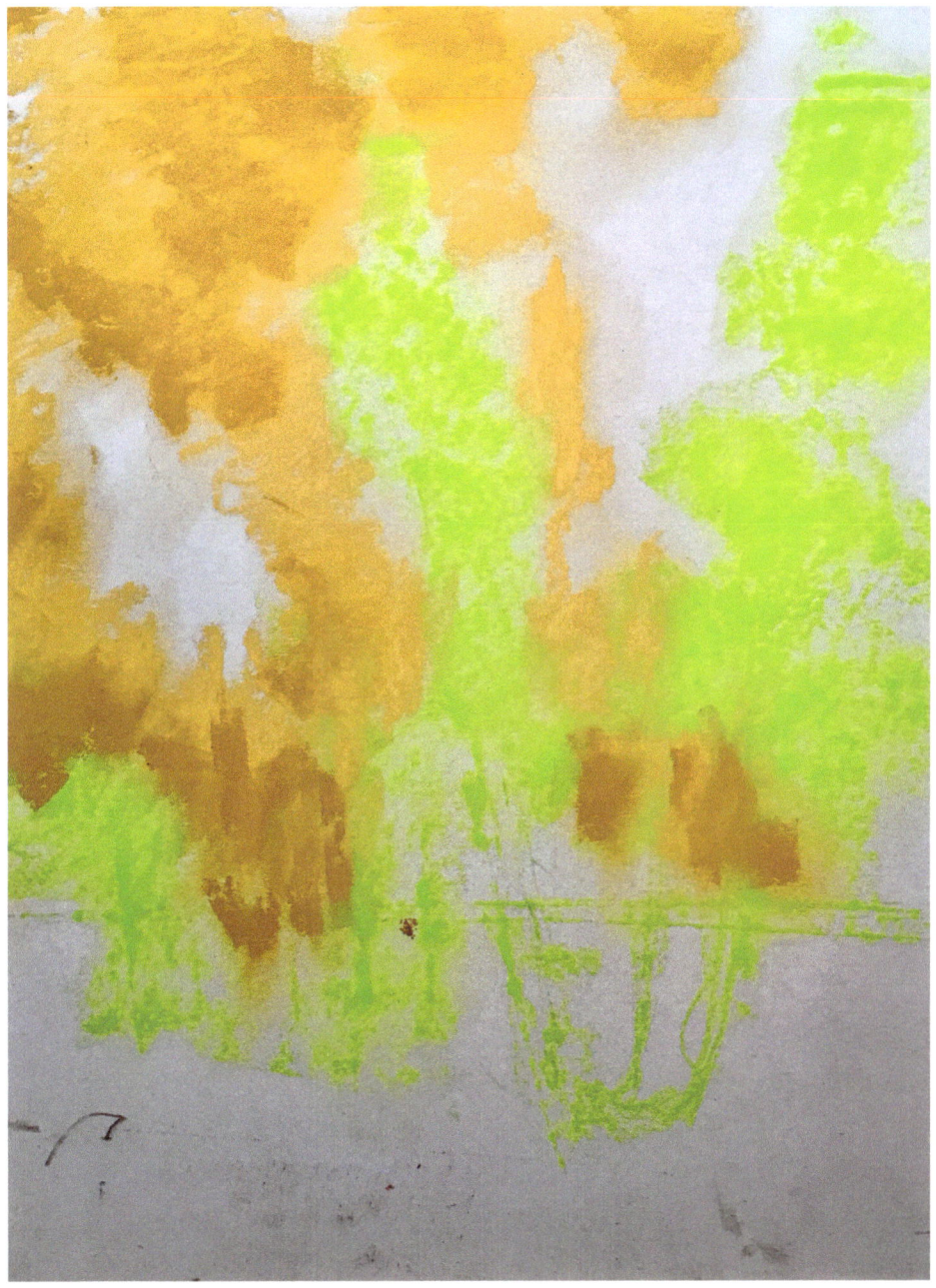

While analyzing your structure, suggest tree trunks with a cool gray. Placement is the importing thing here. We will make color adjustments later.

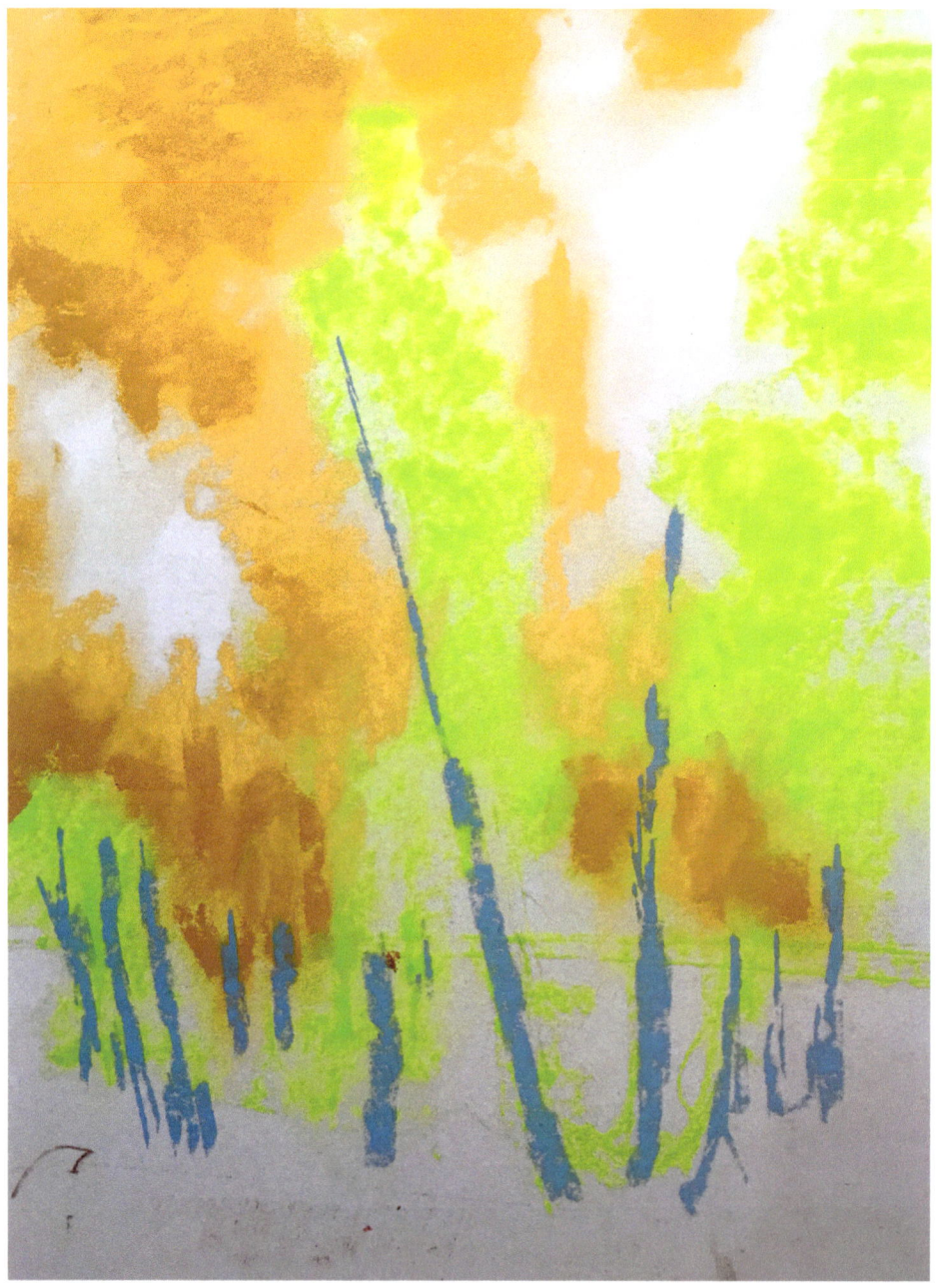

Resist the desire to add detail but give the foreground tree trunks definition. You are working with shallow space but the trunks further back need to show a change in value. Think of this as a building process.

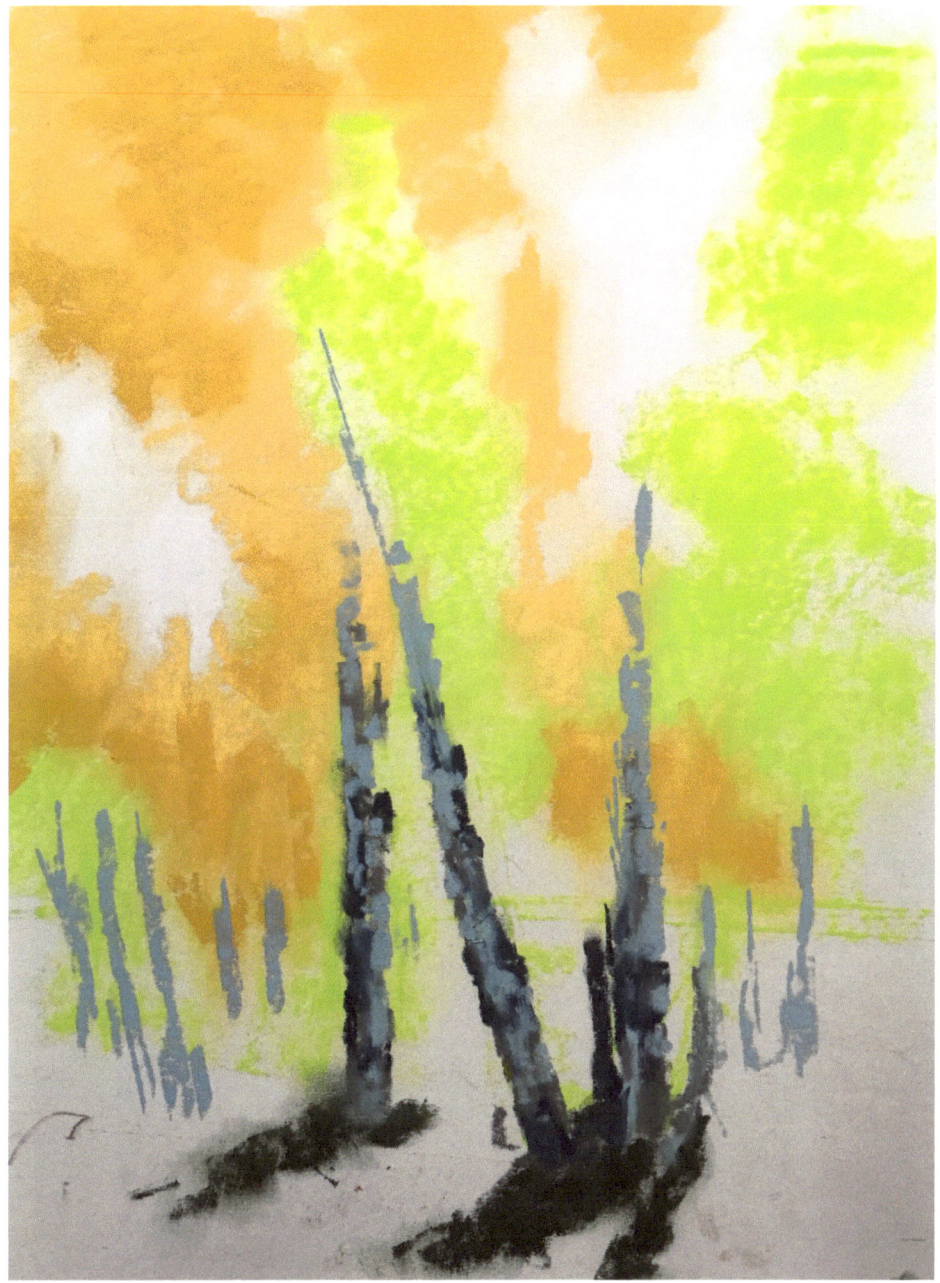

Still resisting the desire to add detail but give the foreground the suggestion of weeds and grasses.

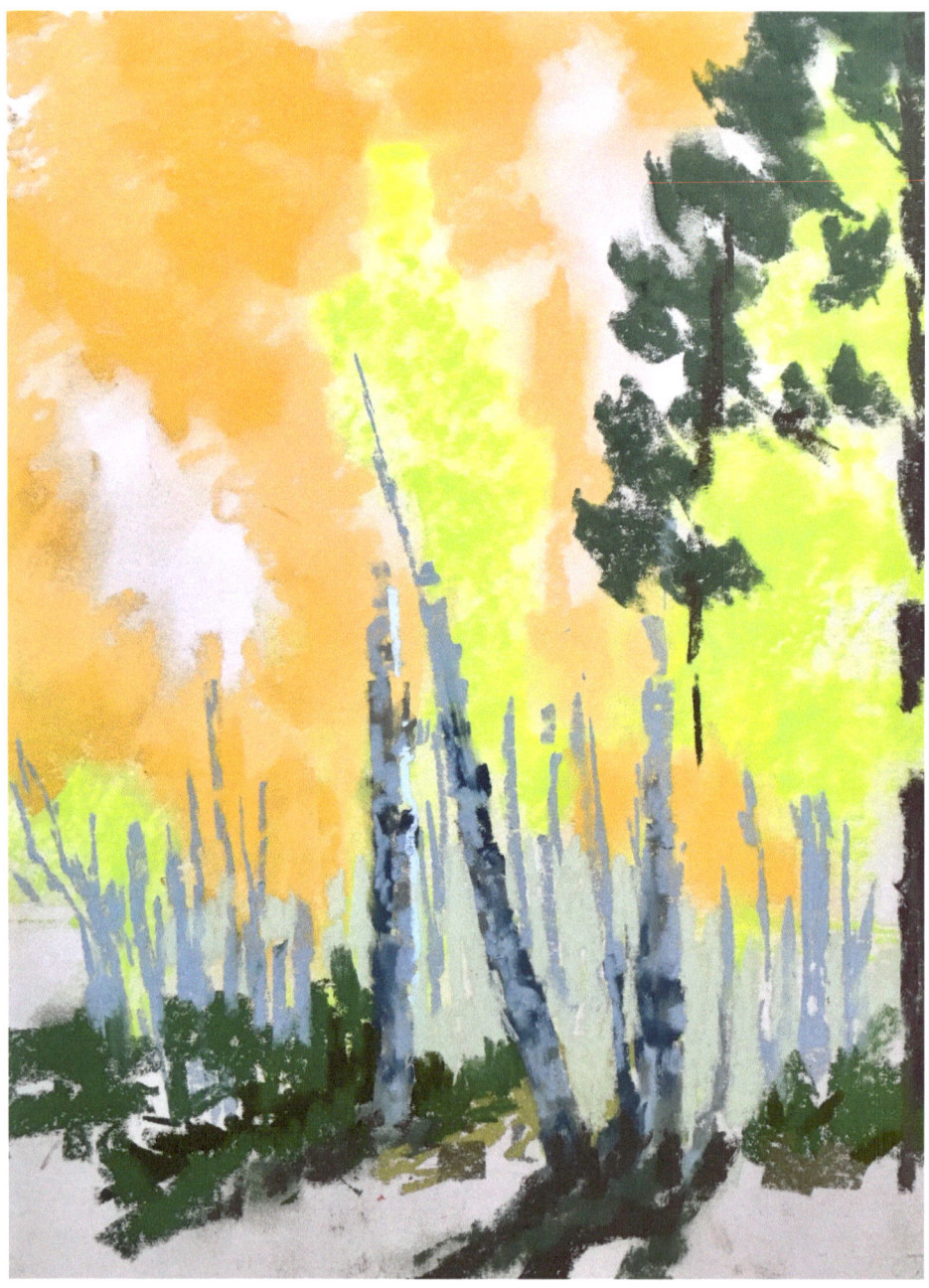

Tree shadows, grasses, and rocks dot the ground and provide us with a visual element to anchor the trees. Notice how abstract the painting begins. Add the suggestion of the fir tree to the right to add a change in texture.

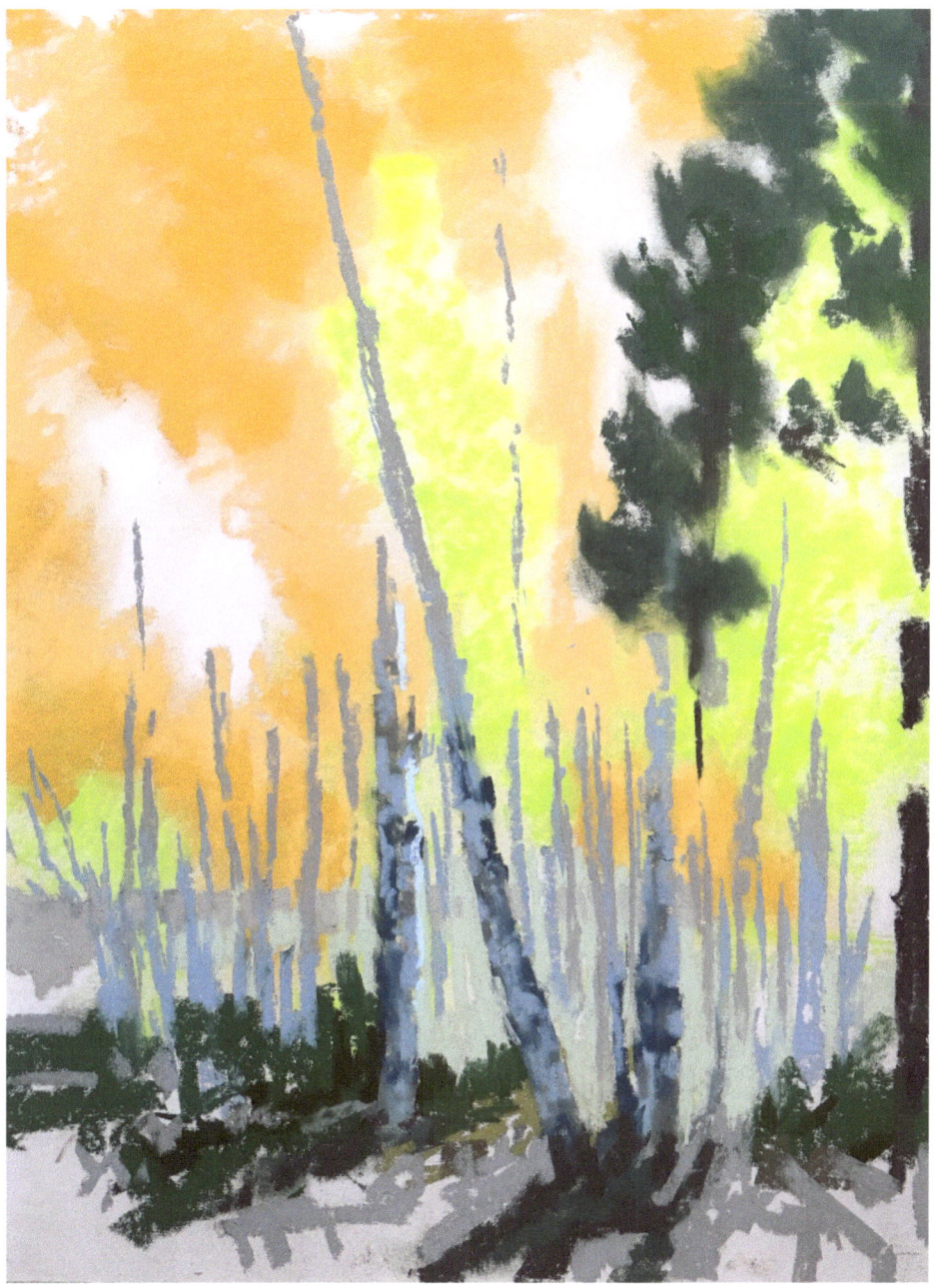

Adding some warm grays to the foreground brings the foreground visually forward. I used the same pastel to cover the ground near the horizon line to keep the ground in a mid-tone while I worked out the composition. Colors play off of each other and look very different depending on their context in the composition. As you look through the images, pay particular attention to the gray.

For a painting to be rich in color and texture you must bravely smudge some of your work and rebuild it. Always back and forth moving toward some detail but never ever starting with detail first. I often use the outside edge of my palm to blend large areas.

Blending the pastels helps create half tones to deepen the range of colors. I enjoy working with pastels because they are opaque and you can keep building. If you need to rid your composition of some unwanted excess just use a paintbrush to brush off the area. This will leave a base mid-tone you can work over. My goal is to use nature as my inspiration but also show my enjoyment of what I see.

This detail of the lower left shows the mosaic of rapidly laid down pastels before blending. You can see that any detail I began to express was obliterated. I am working outside and need to work very fast. The afternoon light behind the Aspen is fading.

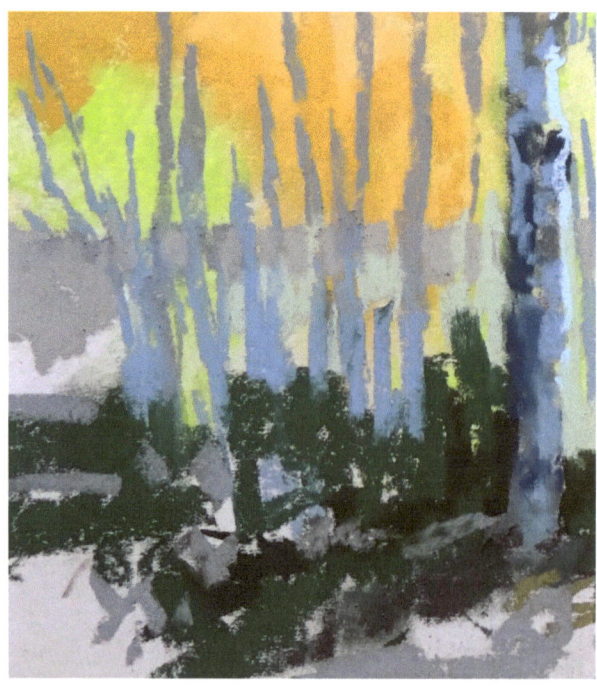

Smudging the pastels, push the pastel dust into the texture of the sanded paper to give it a softer look. I will continue with this process at times throughout the building of the painting.

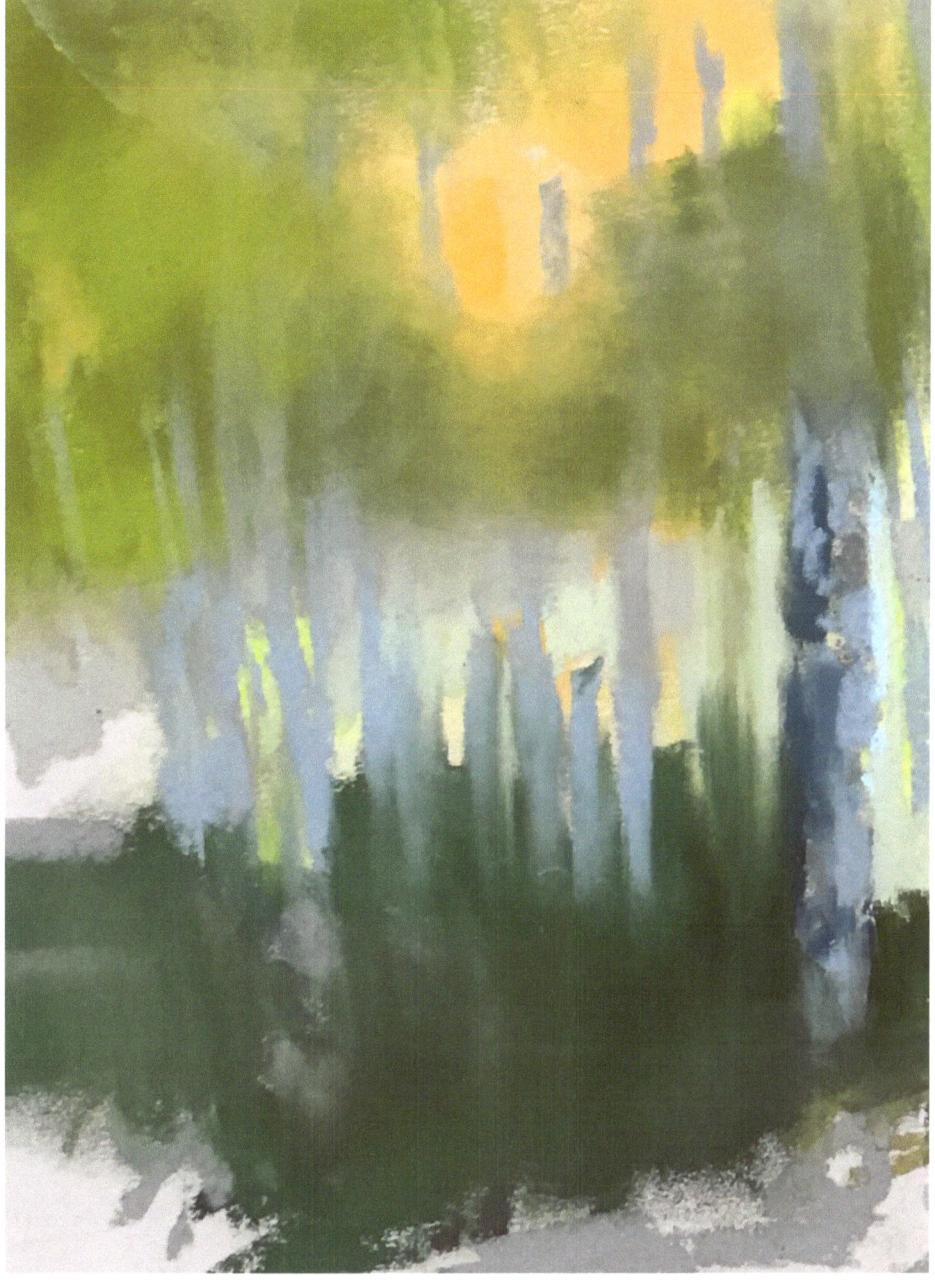

During this blending process, wipe down the page and then wipe the excess off your hand before continuing. This was done after I added green to the lower painting. You want to avoid a muddy mess, only go in a downward direction.

This process of blending, with the edge of my palm, is the way I handle broad areas of blending. I tend to do this at different times throughout my work. Because I work in the field, I use the least amount of supplies possible.

Other artists have their own way, and different working methods help to create individuality in art. Don't be locked into systems of painting and thinking there is only a right or wrong way. Combine what you learn from others and pick and choose ideas that work for you. Some of my students are reluctant to try this because they feel a lack of control, but that is what I like about pastels. Sometimes they have a mind of their own and I want my pastels to look like pastels.

Always keep your pastels you are working with separate from the rest of your pastels. Place them on a tray or box lid, you will be amazed at how difficult it can be to locate one. After you have blended and created these halftones, use this same group of pastels to rework the lighter and darker areas of your painting. Pastel painting is always a process of working and reworking to build a rich and interesting surface and painting.

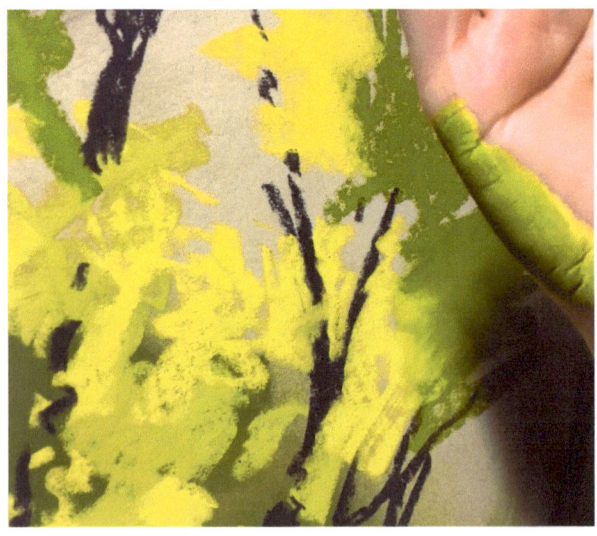

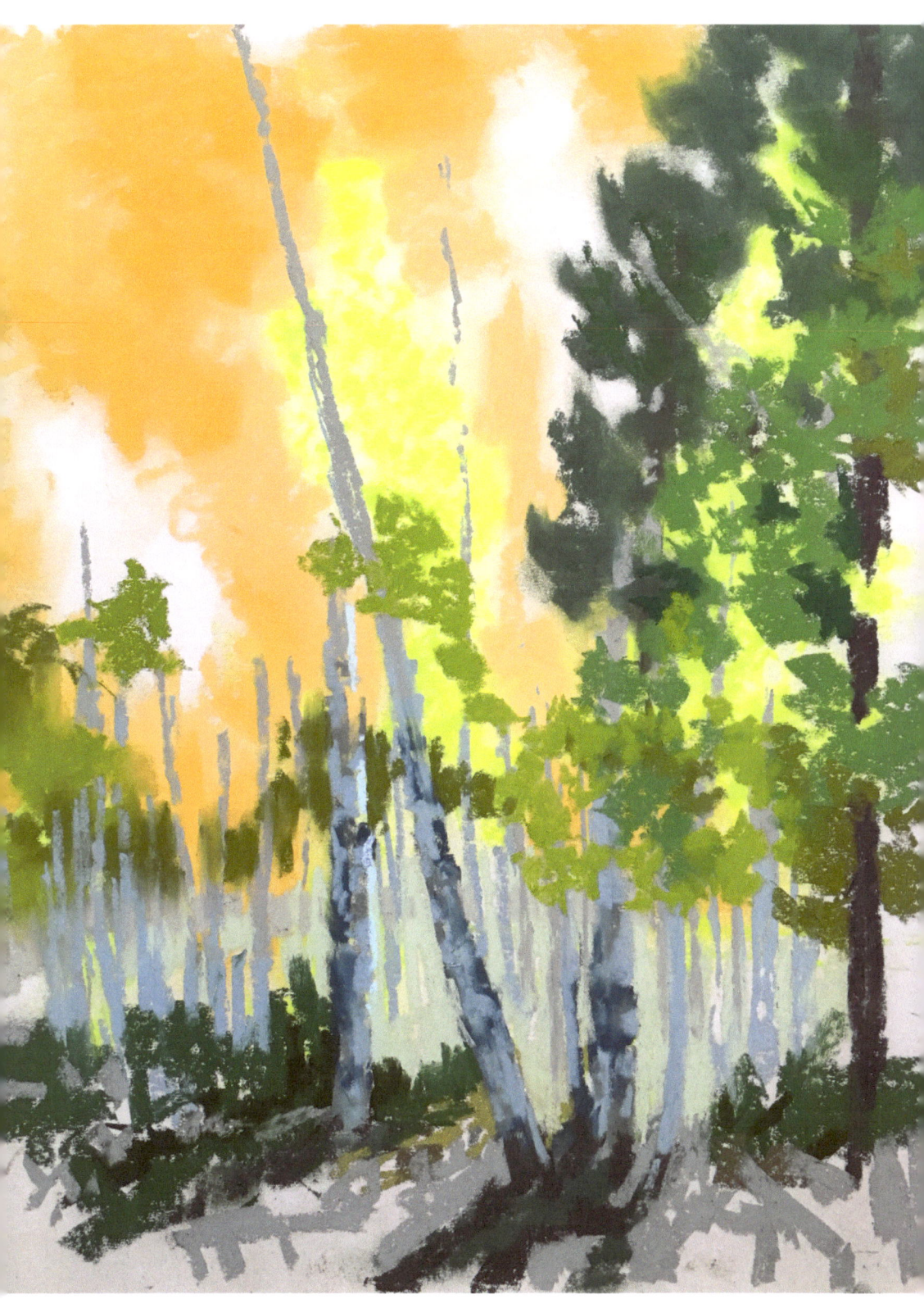

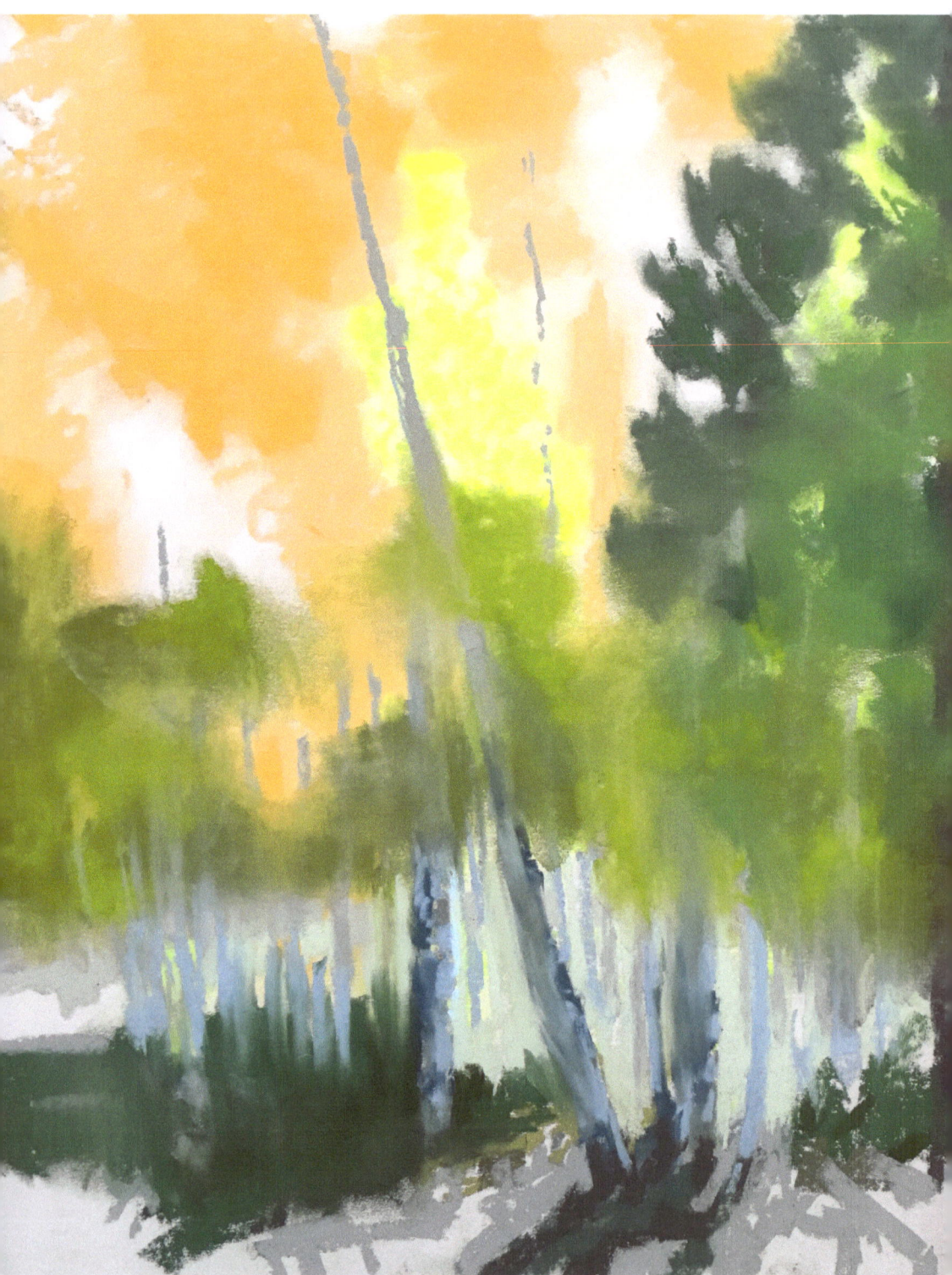

This image is taken after smudging the pastels. Sometimes I use a very soft flat paintbrush, but in this case I used the side palm of my right hand beginning in the middle of the painting and stroking down. Only go in one direction and wipe your palm off for each downward stroke. Always be willing to mess up what you have accomplished in order to get to the next level. This is why you should never waste your time on detail at this point in the painting.

Remember, color is our subject! Therefore, volume, value, line, and form are present but do not dominate your painting. Now that you have created your under-painting, organize your picture space within your picture plane edges and contemplate the beauty of the sun filtering through the Aspen branches. It is time to enhance the color and define your imagery.

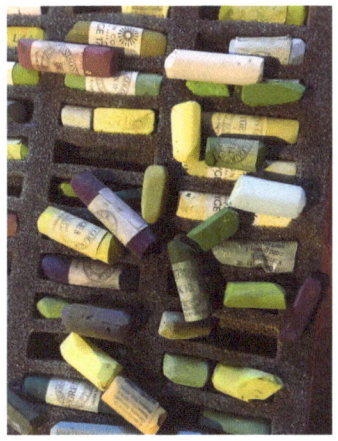

Advanced: After establishing a basic design and color, I begin to use the softer pastels. However, if you are working small, stay with the semi-hard sticks.

SOFT PASTEL BRANDS:
Blue Earth Pastels, Earth Green 28 set.
Unison Half Sticks with 16 Landscape set.
If you can only buy one set to start with, choose this one. Sennelier Half Stick, set 80 Plein Air. This is a great set if you plan to do more work and larger work. Schmincke pastels. I buy these individually.

Most people living in the United States and Western Europe read from left to right; therefore, it is their habit to scan visual imagery in the same way. Often artists use this to help you to navigate through a painting. It is especially prominent in the visual arts for illustrators and graphic designers to use this principle. You are illustrating the beauty of light shining through the tree and you want to share this imagery with others. Otherwise, I would have been content with the memory of the day.

Give some attention to the foreground by blending what you have from the top of the grass to the bottom. This was as far as I got out in the field. The rest was done in my Virginia studio but the memory was with me.

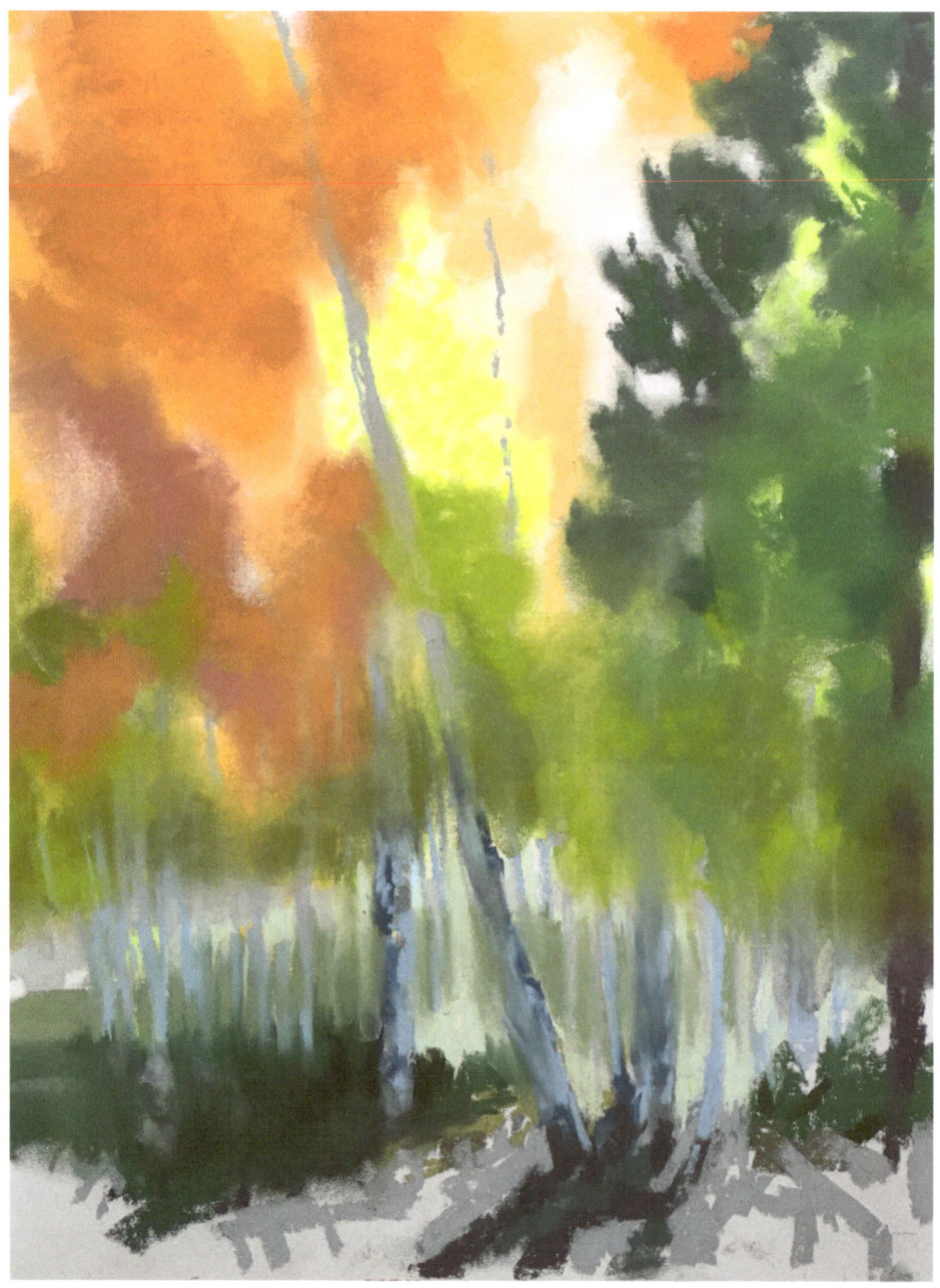

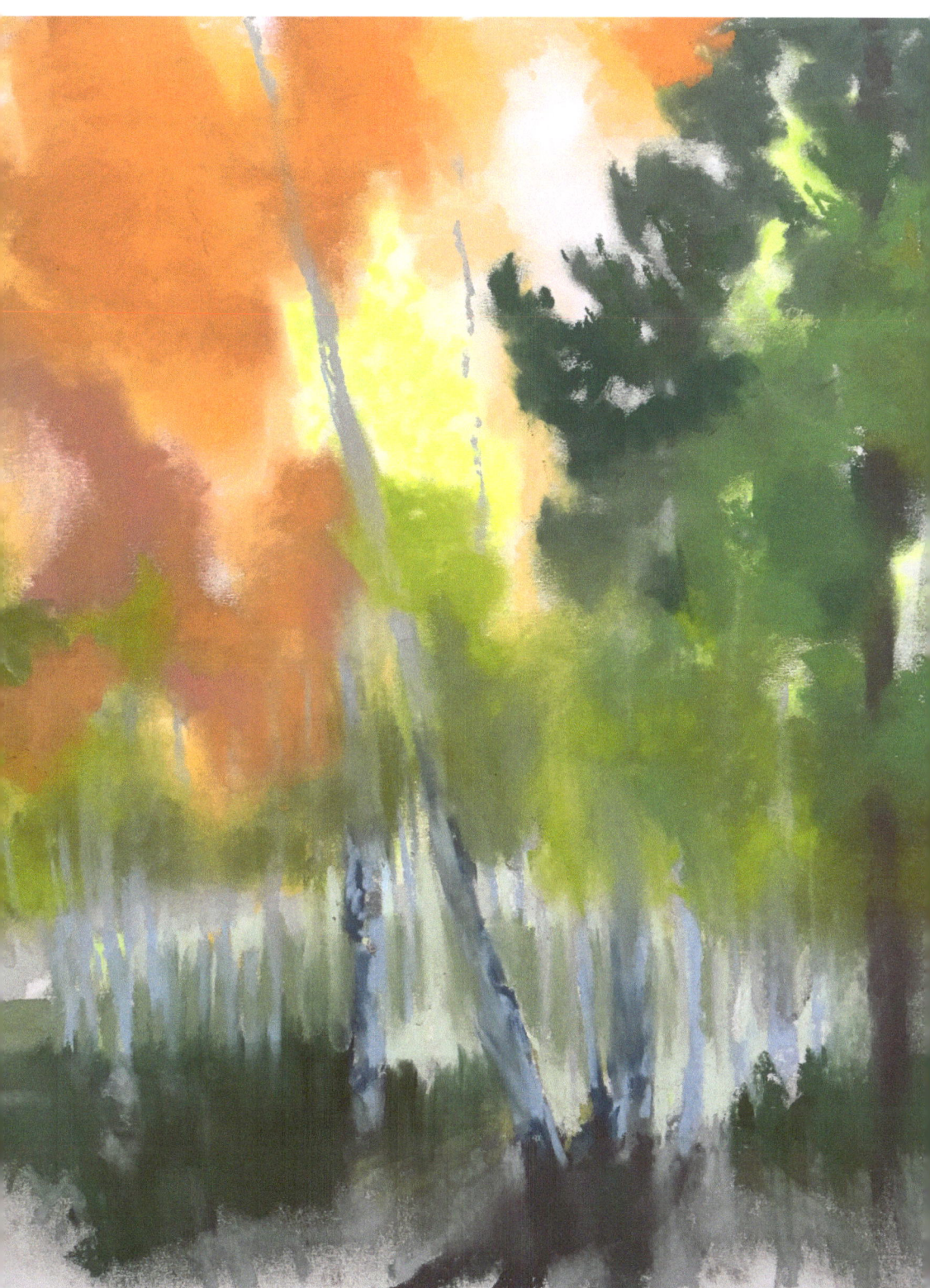

Lighting Hint: I am fortunate to have many windows in my studio, but I use LED Daylight bulbs from Costco to add to the studio lighting (nothing expensive, just standard). You will notice different light changes your color. Working outside in plein air and displaying a painting inside a house often causes important color relationships to be lost. You must be in control of your environment and consider many different lighting options.

The Impressionist realized that some time in the studio to tweak a plein air painting made for a better painting. Studio time allows you the luxury of contemplation. While a camera can capture what is there, the painter must inject their self, their style, and their emotion. Therefore, this painting is an abstract collage of color inspired by nature and the Aspen trees. I spend as much time thinking about the painting as I actually do painting.

At this stage we are adding detail and suggestions of clusters of leaves overlapping bold colors lit by the sun. The soft needles of the pine, the blotchy etched bark of the white Aspen trunks, and the receding ground pushing back under the branches.

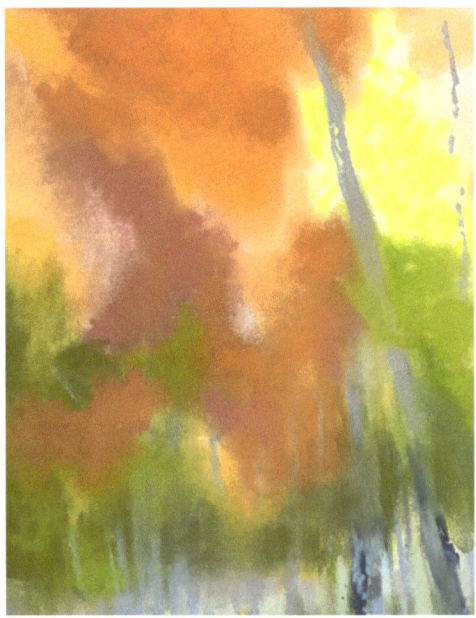

Observe the cooler darker orange. This represents the same orange foliage deeper in the tree that is shaded. This adds a shallow depth to the area rather than everything lying on the same plane. Shallow space requires subtle color changes to hold your design together and allow movement for the viewers' eyes.

Continue adding definition to the foreground; brightening the spaces between the tree trunks where the light is hiding. Begin the definition of the clusters of leaves.

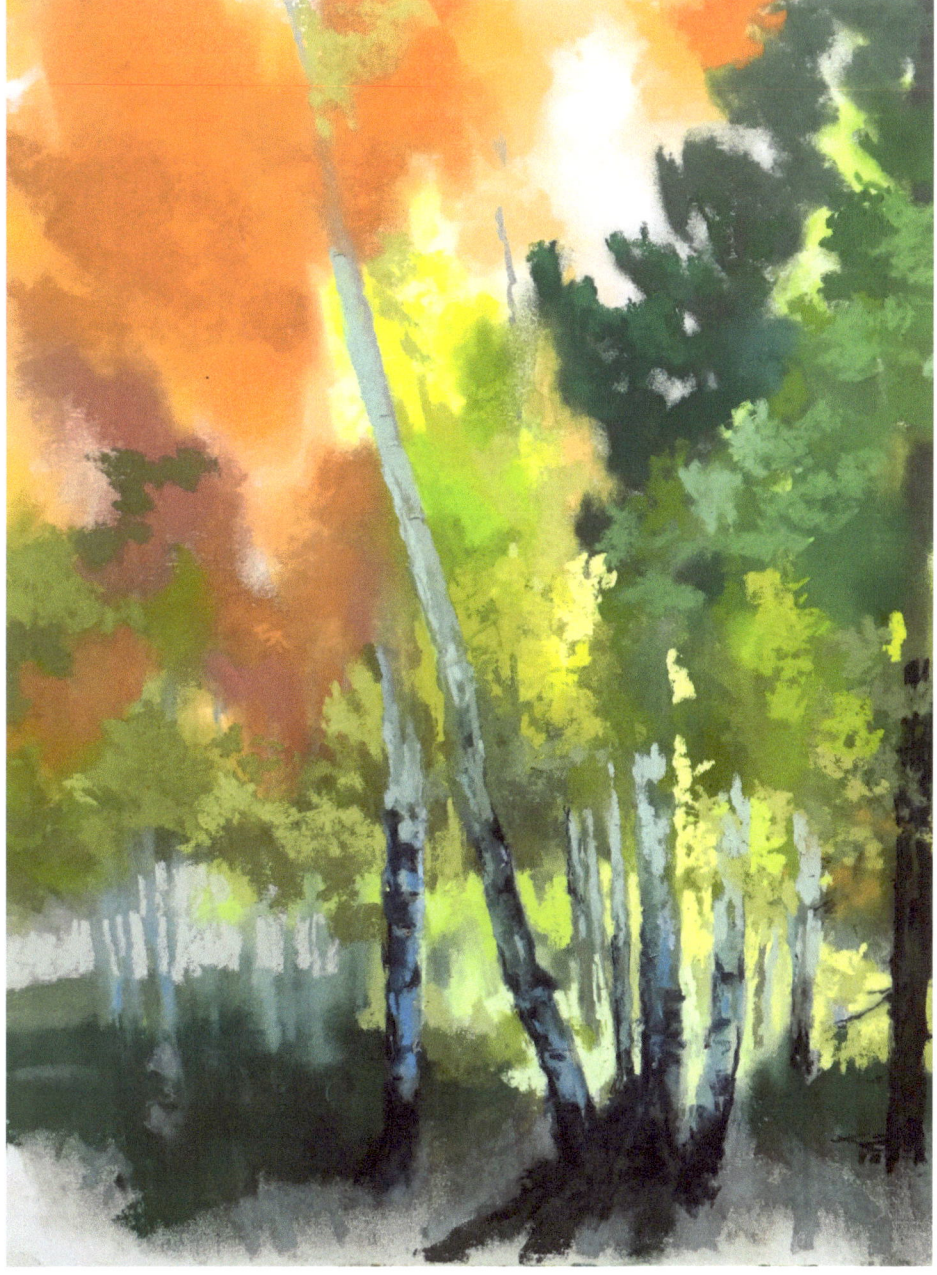

Design and Your Painting

Throughout your painting, you must be mindful of the picture plane design elements, the skeleton that holds together your matrix of color. Because you are working with shallow space, the emphasis for continuity can be achieved by the foreground texture of leaves. Pastel marks suggesting the leaves and flickering light keep the foreground in front while less defined areas of color lead us back through the trees.

I wanted to isolate this portion of the painting to help you remember that you should always strive to utilize both the negative and positive spaces. Notice the bright light color edged along the tree trunks. This color is defining both the tree and leaf edges and is the negative space or shape.

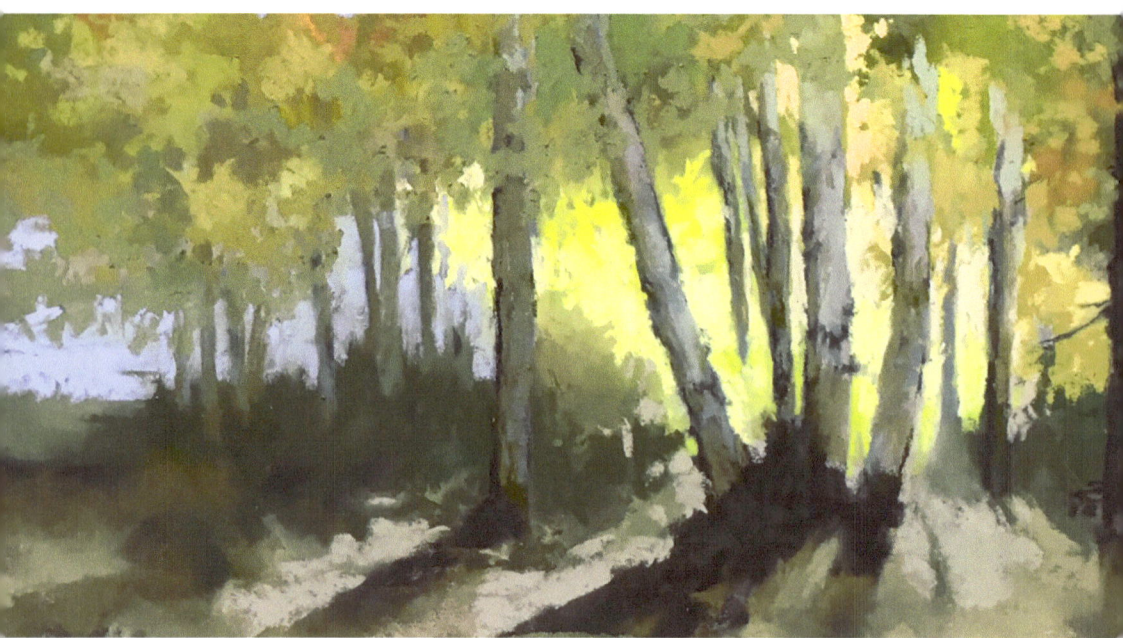

Define all your edges in the foreground by enhancing the light from behind the trees. Remember, cool colors (such as the gray lavender to the left) and the cooler lemon yellow from the winter sun recede and warm colors visually come forward because of their wavelengths. Afternoon sun is usually warm but we need to alter it a bit to make the painting work.

This close-up shows you how I enjoy allowing pastels to be pastels. Pastels are one painting medium that you can't reproduce commercially. You can reproduce the image and that works very well; however, the original is a textured, vibrant collage of pure pigment.

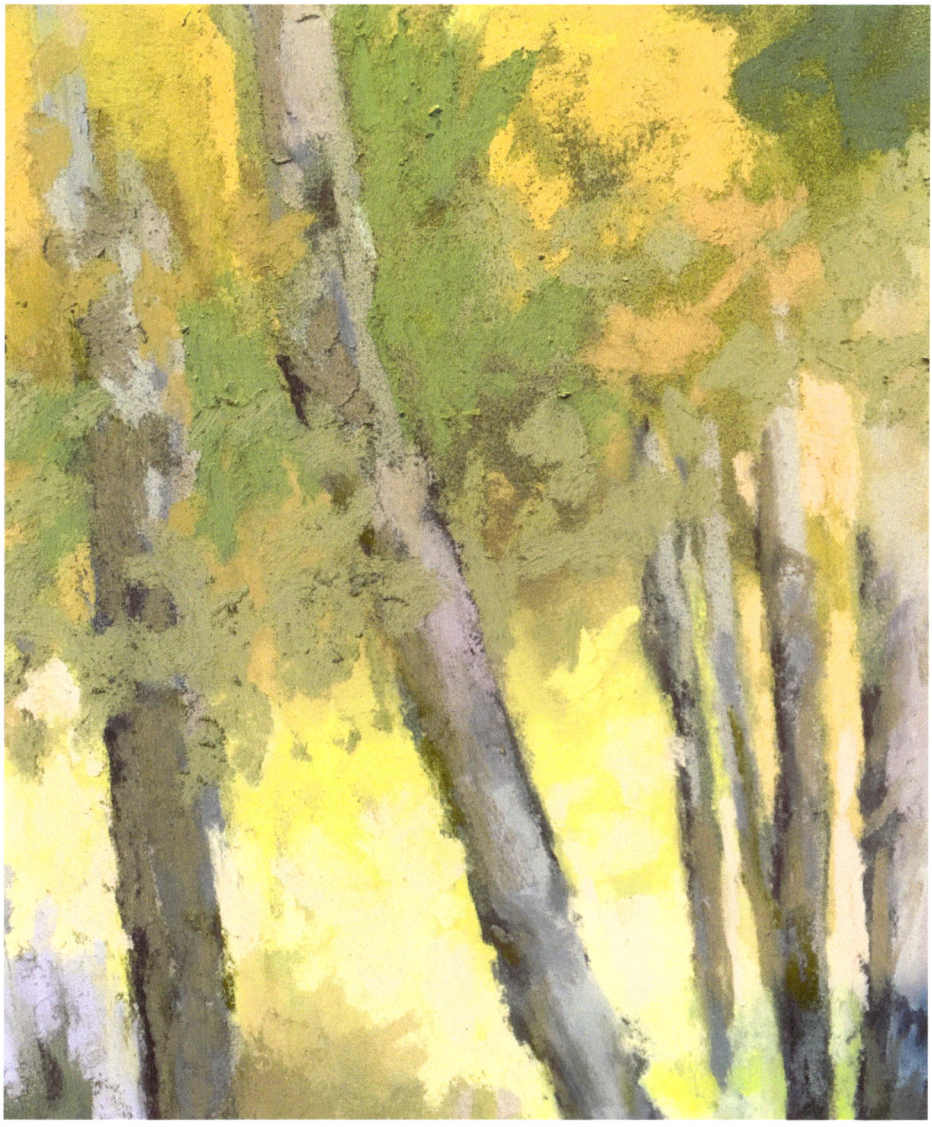

As I grew closer to completing this painting, I snapped this image of the pastel tray. All colors are relative to their surroundings and they will look very different in the box than on the painting. Sometimes this can be a happy mistake because closely related colors make a rich environment.

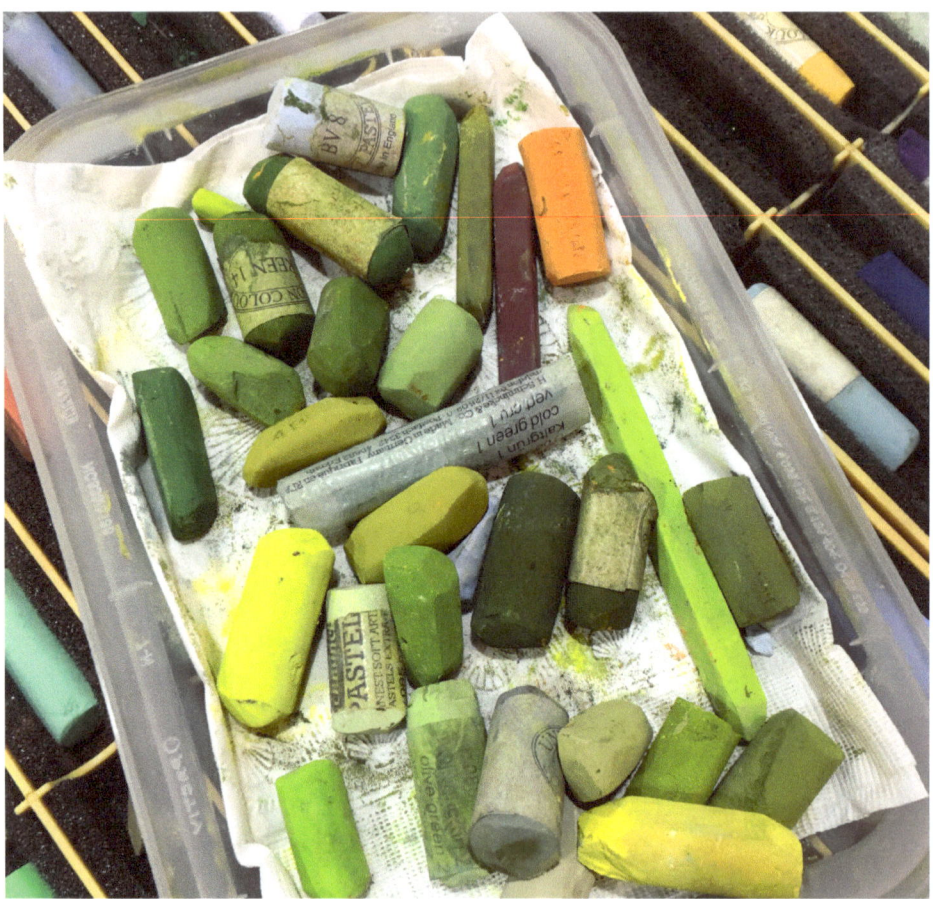

Continue your suggestions of leaves and branches overlapping with light peeking through. The only light on the Aspen trunks is reflected light. The sun is behind the trees so make sure you don't have any bright spots from direct sunlight on the tree trunks.

While working on a piece, I often exhibit the painting in my house where I can walk past and make observations, exploring all areas of the painting and see if something bothers me.

Pastels are worth your trouble to learn because they are just the thing for the busy individual. You can go out and paint with little effort. There is no set up or clean up. Just open the box, close the box, and wash your hands.

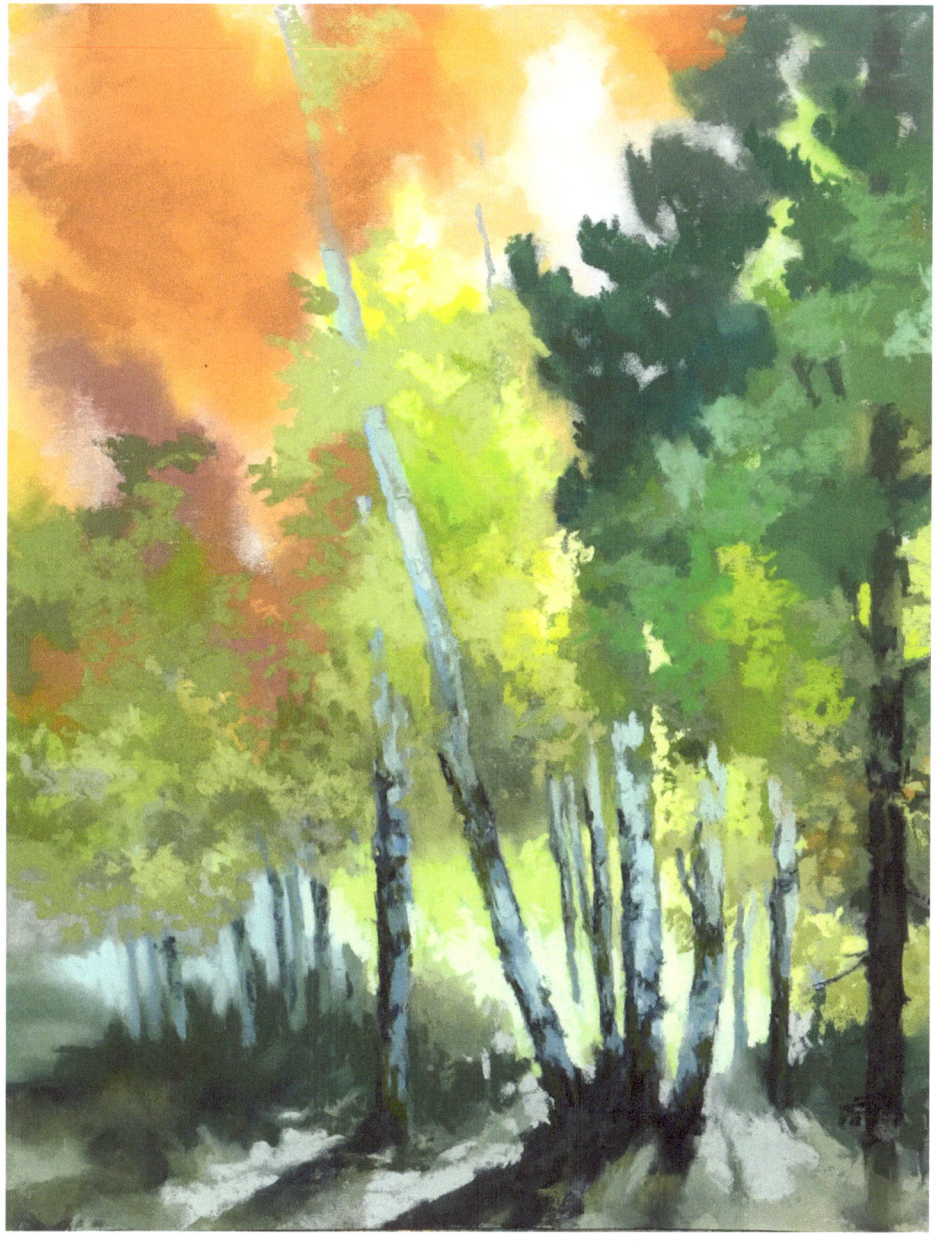

Collect your thoughts

It is the time for close examination of your work and final adjustments. This process will teach you the most about painting, this stage can change your work from good to great.

When you write an essay, you must write quickly while the thoughts are lingering; but after the story has reached its initial conclusion, most writers give it a final polish.

You have created an essay with color and line, which requires the same attention.

Is your color what you want it to be because this painting is about color!

Have you used your negative space to create a reveling edge where the tree foliage meets the filtering low sunlight. This area is important because it pulls you into the space of the painting and you can travel past the vertical aspen trunks.

Be sure to examine your sky holes again; without them you are visually blocked by a solid wall of undefined color. These few simple shapes of sky allow you to read the trees as what they are meant to be in the painting.

In painting, each mark with the pastel or brush must be considered for its relevance to the whole by value, color, shape, and context. It may appear random but it is not. Like the right word in your essay, you need the right color.

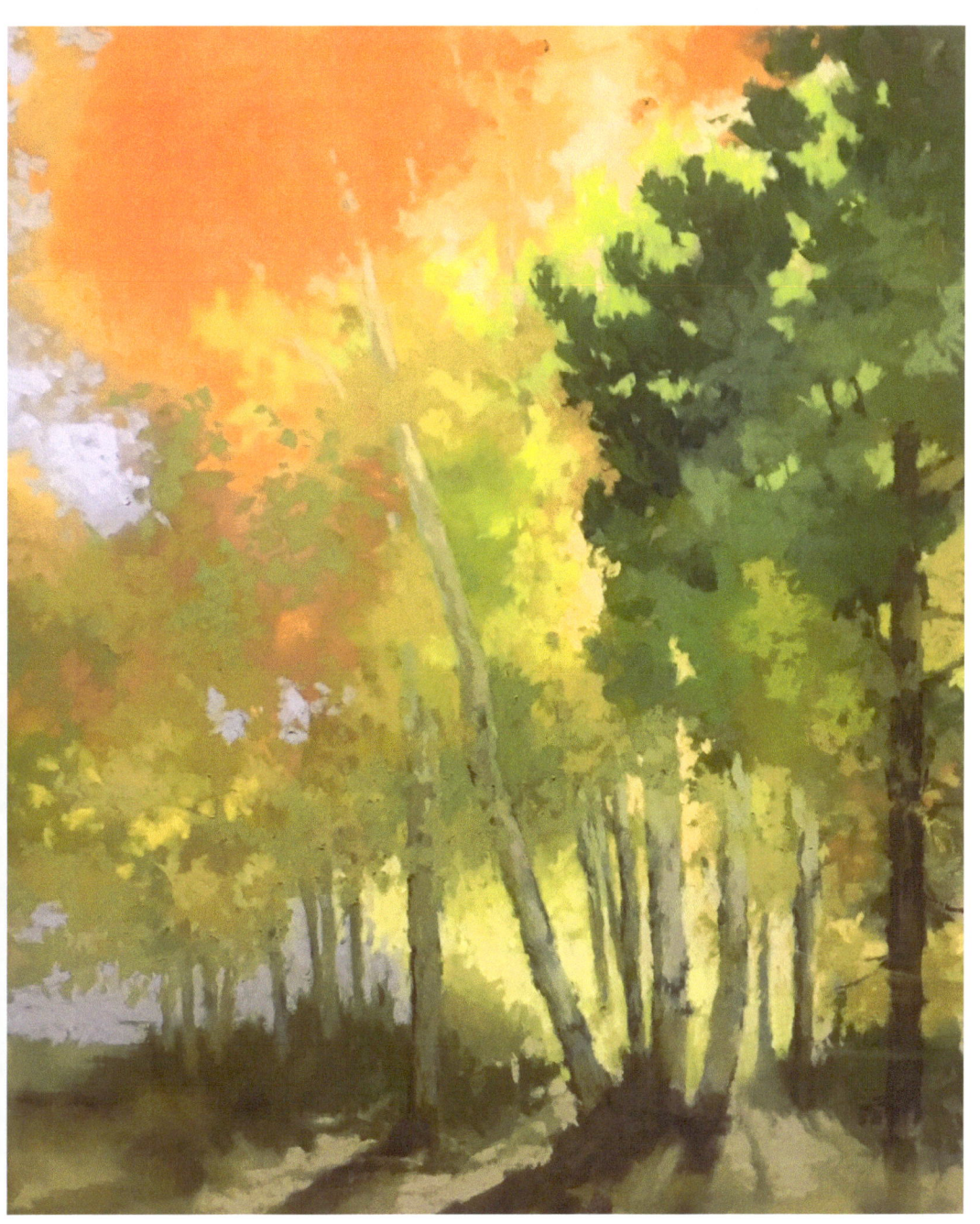

The arts teach us to make good judgments about qualitative relationships. Unlike a curriculum in which correct answers and rules prevail, in the arts, it is judgment rather than rules that prevail.
— Elliot Eisner

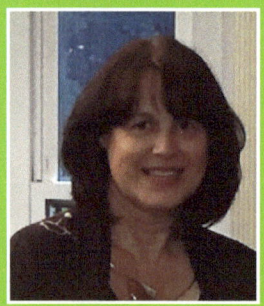

I would like to thank my husband and family for their love of "out in nature" places and joining me.

A special thank you to the artists at the Escalante Canyons Art Festival for hosting their annual Plein Air event. Escalante's location along Utah's Scenic Byway 12 brought me to American landscapes I will never forget. *Escalantecanyonsartfestival.org*

I hope you have enjoyed this lesson in working with pastels and will continue to explore nature around you. Sit quietly on a log listening to the sounds of nature, and paint what inspires you.

Your world will feel better, and your smile will be brighter.
— Alexia

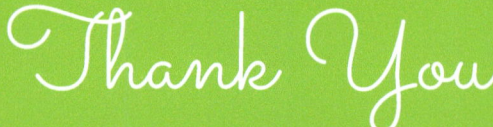

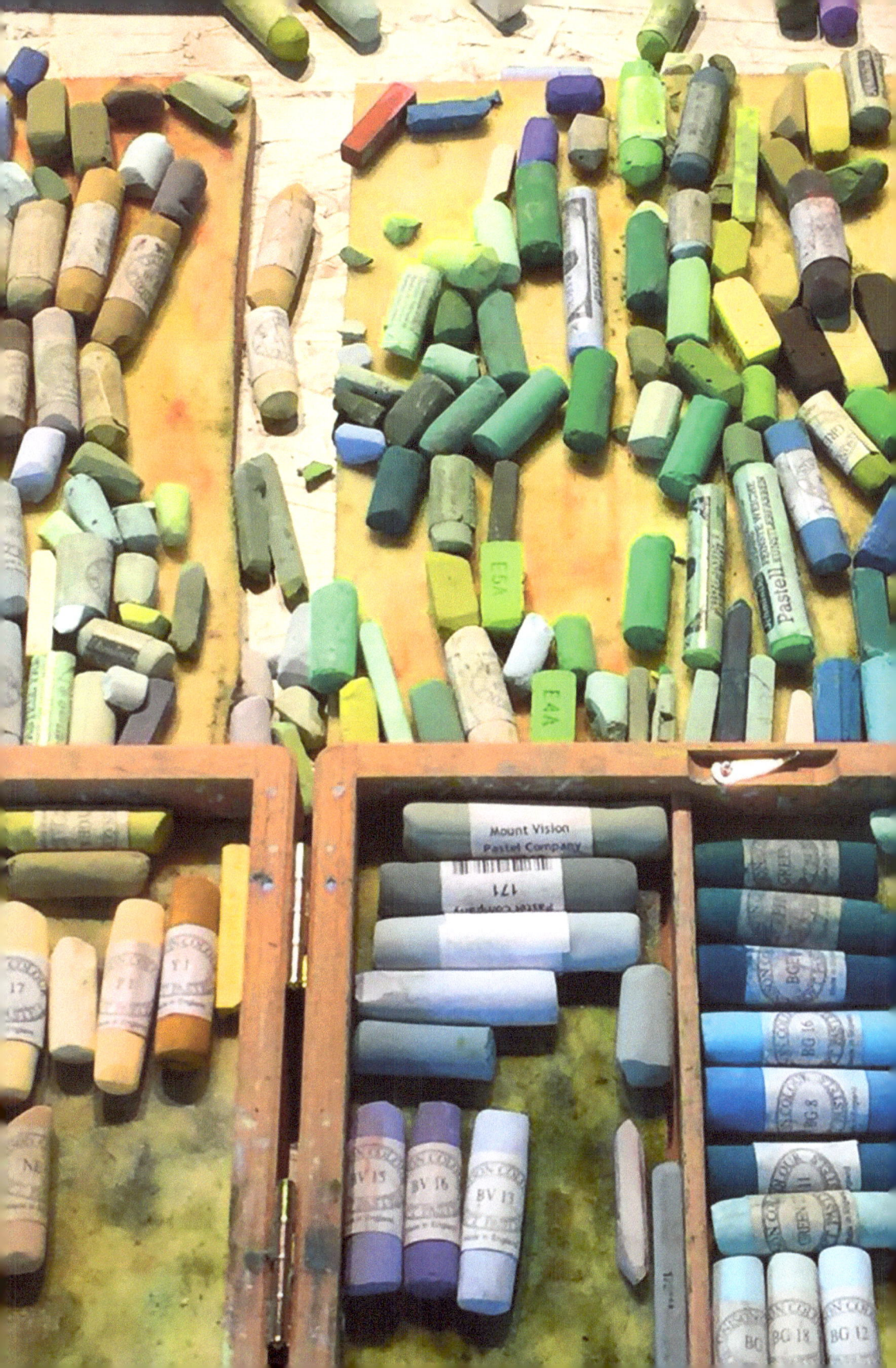

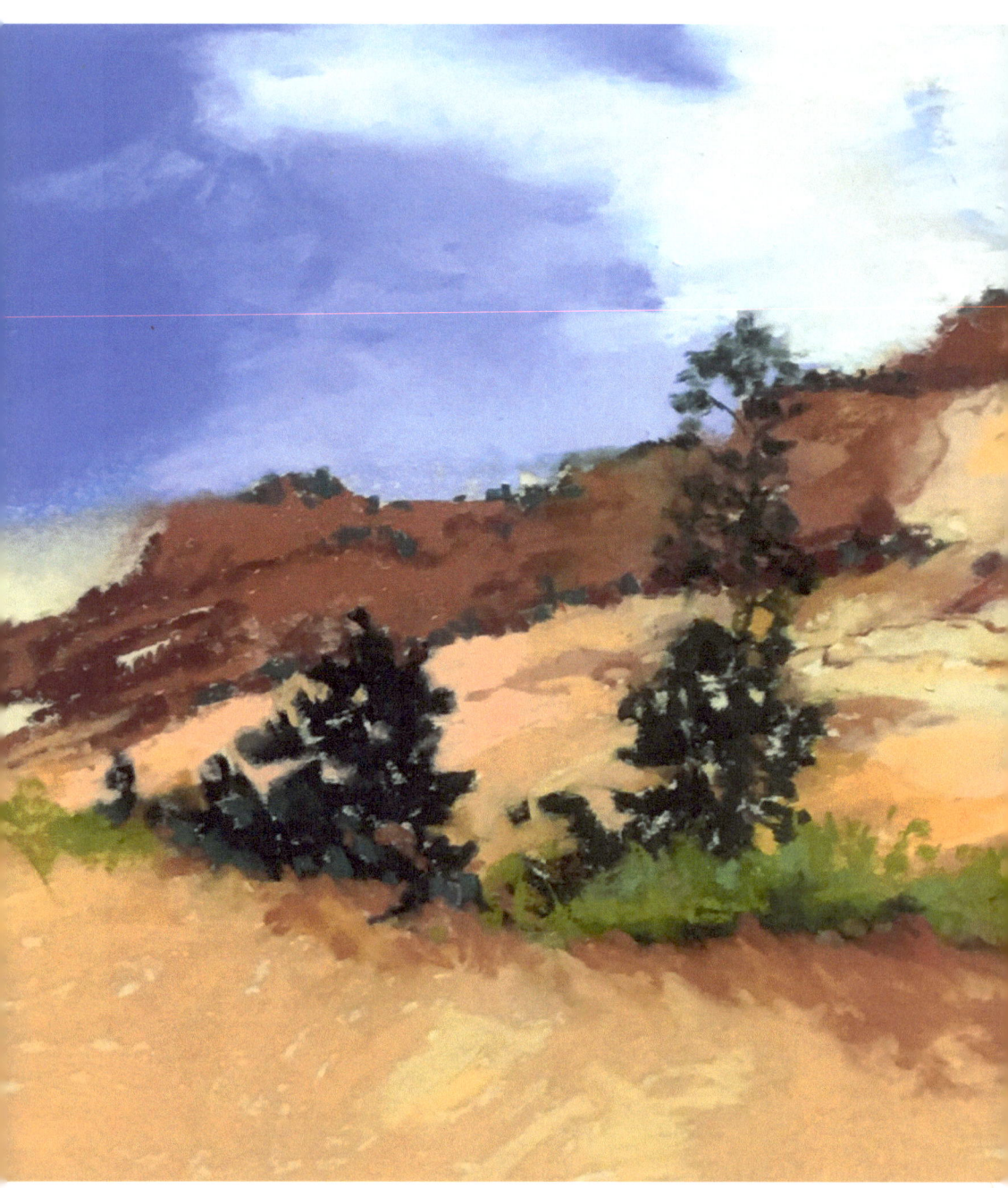

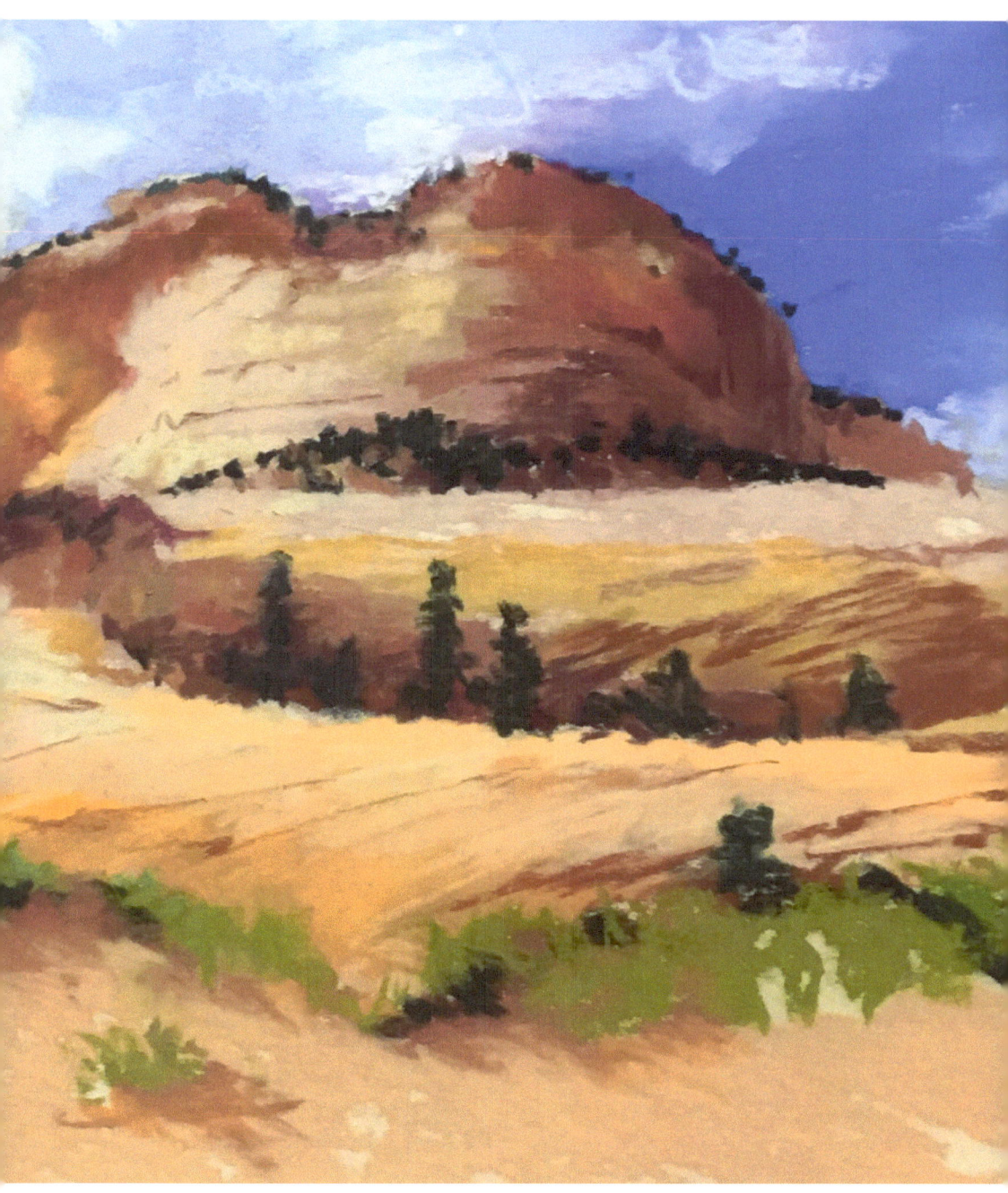

When we returned home to Virginia, our beautiful Sugar Maple was just beginning its fall journey. This pastel painting is also backlit like the Aspen.

By following what you have learned so far, give this one a try or pick a pastel image from my website. There is no substitute for time spent working and creating color relationships.

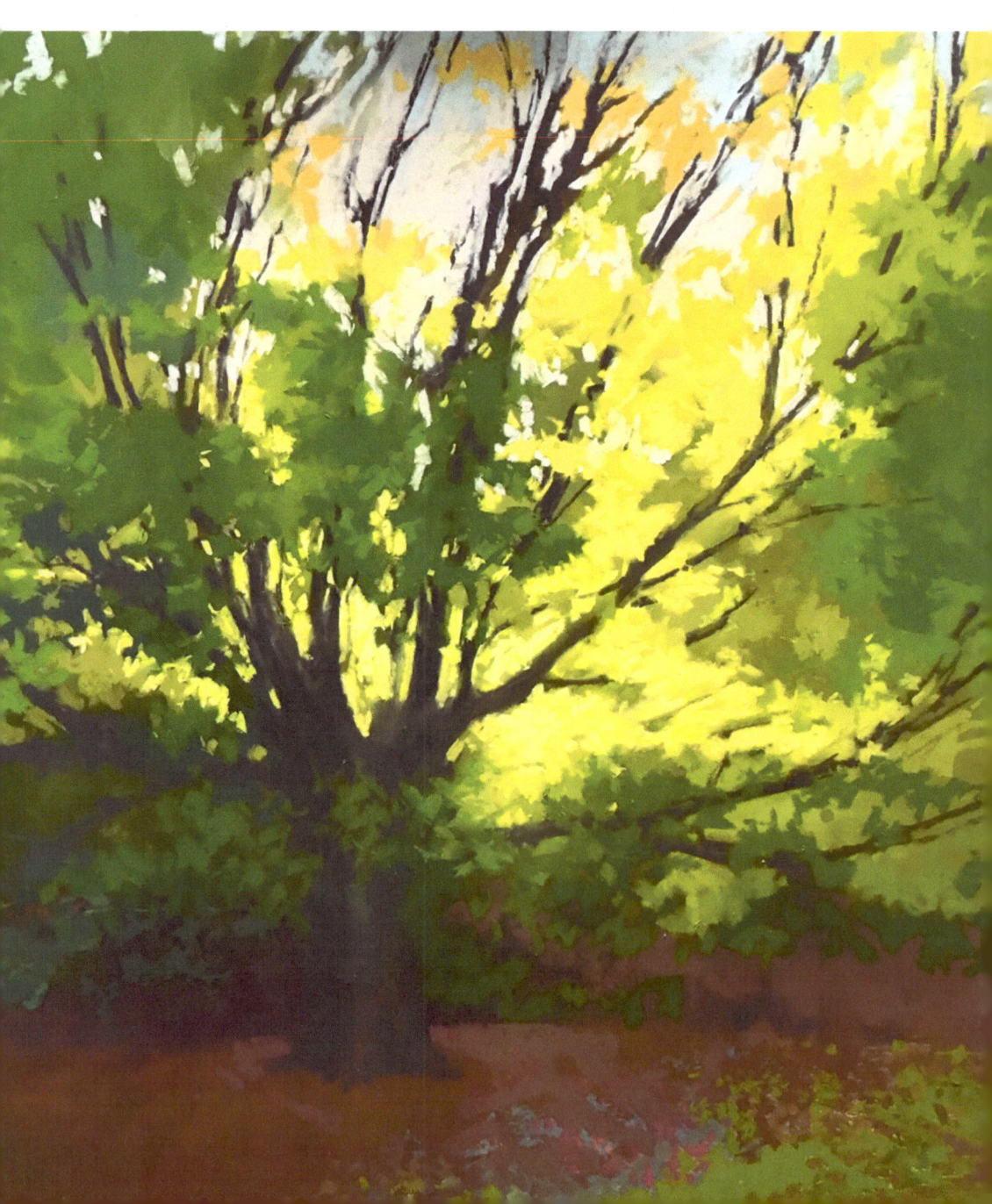

www.ingramcontent.com/pod-product-compliance
Lightning Source LLC
Chambersburg PA
CBHW040923180526
45159CB00002BA/589